D0611586

The HOPE Of HEAVEN

BT
902
.067
1988

Oppenheimer, Helen,
1926-

    The hope of heav-
en

THE HOPE OF HEAVEN
What Happens When We Die?

Helen Oppenheimer

1 9 8 8

Cowley Publications
Cambridge, Massachusetts

★ ★ ★ ★

Forward Movement Publications
Cincinnati, Ohio

© 1988 by Helen Oppenheimer. All rights reserved.
Published in the United States of America by Cowley
Publications
and Forward Movement Publications
Published in Great Britain by Fount paperbacks.
International Standard Book No. 0-936384-56-5

Library of Congress Cataloging-In-Publication Data

Oppenheimer, Helen, 1926 -
 The hope of heaven: what happens when we die?/Helen
 Oppenheimer
 160 pages cm
 British ed. published as: Looking before and after
 Bibliography: p. 156
 ISBN: 0-936384-56-5 $7.95
 1. Future life—Christianity. I. Title.
 BT 902.067 1988
 236'.2—dc19

                                                87-33120
                                                CIP

To
Jennifer and Desmond

Contents

Foreword

by the Archbishop of Canterbury

Delicacy of style and precision in the use of language are well attested features of Helen Oppenheimer's writings. In this book she uses these gifts to great effect in helping us to reflect upon our humanity and our worth before God. As with the best sermons, we begin to realize the truth about ourselves and about God without recognizing how gently we have been guided into territories of thought we rarely inhabit.

Wherever the Christian faith makes a profound impact upon society it is intellectually alive as well as pastorally effective. A careful blend of both features is found in these pages. I hope this book will make all who read it think, and that the imaginative and carefully chosen reflections at the end of each chapter will ensure that thinking leads into prayer.

I am grateful to Helen Oppenheimer for agreeing to write this book, and am sure my gratitude will be shared by all who read it.

Preface

This book nibbles at a huge subject, the nature and destiny of human beings. It is written for Christians who want to love God with their minds, in the hope of showing that thinking need not mean worrying. There is quite a lot about death, but very little about sin, even less about society, and only too little about God Himself, simply because it is best to pursue one discussion at a time.

I have used some sentences from a sermon on "Life after death" preached in the University of Oxford in February 1979 and printed in *Theology* the following September, by kind permission of the Vice-Chancellor and of the Editors of *Theology*. Otherwise none of the book has appeared in print. I have made some use of two papers I wrote for the Inter-Anglican Theological and Doctrinal Commission, and of another paper for a small group set up under the auspices of the Foundation for the Study of Christianity and Society.

I am especially grateful to people who have set me thinking on these subjects by asking me to give talks: particularly to Ronald Coppin, Canon of Durham, for inviting me to talk to junior clergy; and to Reggie Askew, Principal of Salisbury and Wells Theological College, for asking me to lecture in the College: both agreeable occasions with delightful hospitality.

Philip and Elizabeth Turner, on a visit from New York, kindly read some chapters and made helpful comments.

My best thanks once again are due to my husband, to whose kind and practical encouragement in many ways I owe more than I can say.

Helen Oppenheimer

Sure he that made us with such large discourse
Looking before and after, gave us not
That capability and god-like reason
To fust in us unused. . . .

Hamlet Act IV Scene 4

1

A Cluster of Questions

What are we?

There are a number of unfinished arguments going on about the nature and value of human beings. Some of us keep on asking questions about souls and people, the material and the spiritual, identity, minding and mattering, death and resurrection. It still seems both possible and important to try to find out about what used to be called "the end of man"; whether there is any ultimate purpose in life; and whether it still makes sense – and if so, what sense – to affirm that we are made in God's image. The arguments sometimes illuminate, sometimes confuse, the total picture. They need to be pursued both separately and together, because what looks like an answer to one question is apt to turn out to be a formidable obstacle to resolving another. There is no harm in lumping all the questions together under the heading of "the soul", provided that "soul" is the name of a set of problems not of a solution to them.

The starting point ought to be gratitude for freedom to enter into these arguments with remarkably little risk of persecution, whether violent for religious conviction or social for eccentricity. English-speaking people in the late twentieth century can be Christian or sceptical, orthodox or heretical, traditional or radical, without losing their lives, their jobs, or even their reputations.

In our times thinking may be patient, accurate, clear, interesting: but it will hardly ever deserve to be

13

praised as "courageous". One is allowed to pursue an argument where it goes, to feel the confusion of being on both sides at once, the salutary consciousness that slogans are only names of problems, the excitement of making progress and even coming to conclusions, and the stimulation of seeing further problems open up like a mountain landscape. One has seldom been so free to get into muddles of one's own choosing.

The difficulty in all this freedom is to keep hold of the fact that somewhere in the muddles there is truth not of one's own choosing, maybe simple, maybe complex, maybe beyond one's understanding, but anyway not at one's disposal. Not all questions are for us to decide. Freedom is a matter of where and how to explore, not of what we may find.

There is a different kind of difficulty in this variegated and overgrown territory: to keep the exploration straightforward enough that it does not become a private journey that nobody else will join. It is just as well still to hear the voice of the maths teacher of one's childhood reiterating "show your workings", rather than simply to forge ahead hoping to arrive somewhere eventually. The first step is to pose some questions plainly, even if they sound naïve, and even if we cannot expect to go very far towards thorough answers to them. We need them as signposts into the complexity.

What we want is to make the multiplicity of questions cluster round a nucleus, and the ancient idea of "the soul" is a convenient nucleus. Does it still make sense to talk about souls at all? Are souls immortal? Or is death the end of us? Is it their souls that somehow make human beings intrinsically sacred? And what has sacredness to do with excellence?

These questions about "the soul", that is about human durability, human sacredness, human excellence, are practical questions, though they may develop complicated theoretical ramifications. They are asked by people who want to know what is going to happen to them and how they ought to live. If the practical concern is submerged the real questions are lost, not clarified.

At about this stage we are urged by philosophers, disastrously I believe, to keep fact and value separate. Of course facts and values are easily confused and need to be distinguished, but we shall only impoverish our thinking if we try to keep them apart in a kind of quarantine. It is quite sophisticated to think of facts as "value-free" and values as something to be added in later; and "sophisticated" can mean "spoilt" as well as "mature". We can spoil our humanity by trying to be so cool, calm and collected that we leave everything that really matters out of the real world.

Fact and value are linked in our own selves if anywhere. We must find a way of asking something like the portmanteau question "What is man?" For several reasons we are uncomfortable with that question nowadays, but it is not so easy to get rid of it. At least we can ask it carefully, wary of the assumptions packed up in it.

First there is an assumption to be repudiated: that "man" means only "men". Of course we know perfectly well that "man" is correct English for the whole human race, including men and women; but it allows people to feel, and eventually even to think, that women are subsidiary. The question "What is man?" will no longer do just as it stands, not because it is really unclear but because it moulds people's minds. It is insidiously diminishing to both men and women to be tacitly invited to think of maleness as somehow more fundamentally human than femaleness.

Secondly there is an assumption to be accepted: that it is worth trying to ask the old inanity. "What are we?" is not just bogus. "Humanity" is something. There is some sense in talking about human nature and even in asking whether human life has a purpose. In other words, "What is man?" is not to be translated impatiently into "What are people?", with the implication that the answer would be "Butchers and bakers and candlestick makers". What is being looked for is a way of answering which might pick out the distinctive character of humanity, whether as created or evolved or both. Are we really of more value than many sparrows? And is there anything about us which can endure? What I am assuming is that these questions are not merely silly.

Two ways of answering

Yet strangely enough, Christians of all people are sometimes inhibited from positive answers to questions about human worth. They have assumptions about what the Christian faith is, which make it seem shocking to say that such poor fallen creatures as we are have any kind of value. There is more unpacking to be done.

God both makes the world and saves it: that is an extremely simple statement of the Christian faith. Making and saving are two fundamental ways of talking about God, and at first sight there is no particular problem about putting these two ideas alongside one another. They are not in rivalry. They are both part of the same story: that creation is "very good"; that it is marred by sin and evil; that God's love is unalterable and that He has made atonement at great cost; and that He will bring everything to perfection. There is no clash between the ideas of creating the world and redeeming it: quite the contrary. They are both ideas about what it means to say that God is love.

Yet there is a puzzling split here: not in the basic

16

outline of the Christian faith, but in the worlds of values we discover when we develop separately the two notions of making and saving. In the one way of thinking, God is glorified by His manifold works and the earth is full of His riches.[1] In the other way of thinking, creatures are fragile and in poor shape, all unworthy of His care. Characteristically Christians have emphasized most of all the saving, the redemption of the world by our Lord Jesus Christ. Christianity is, above all, a religion of undeserved grace. Our God is the God who humbled Himself even to death on a cross: who died for sinners, not for worthy, virtuous people. So the kind of love that imitates the love of Christ, the love that was given the new name "agape", does not demand excellence in the beloved but treats every one of God's children, however insignificant or damaged, as sacred and inviolable. Whatever else we go on to say, if we are Christians this way of looking at the world has to be of literally crucial importance.

At this point the glory of creation begins to go by default. The values of making seem to lapse into insignificance. When God's love for the unworthy is the burden of our song, we hardly dare sing with the same emphasis that "the Lord shall rejoice in his works".[2] We may well ask, "What is man that Thou art mindful of him?", and we know that the answer is "Thou madest him lower than the angels: to crown him with glory and worship".[3] But Christians easily feel obliged to shrink this answer to mean one special Man only. So the glory and worship are ascribed entirely to Christ's saving love, not to the humanity we share with him as made in God's image. The wretchedness of ourselves and our fellow human beings, not the splendour in store for us, can seem to be the whole point. Our creed is supposed to be simply contrary to "humanism".

It may be quite bluntly said that this is a pathetic

impoverishment of the Christian faith. God is not magnified by the inadequacy of His creatures but by their ultimate excellence, and we have some foretastes of that excellence even in the world we know. Unless creation is wonderful, redemption cannot amount to much either. The Cross itself shows the value of human beings. Sinners as we know we are, this is what we are worth in God's sight.[4]

The mention of "humanism" could have set us on a wrong track, as if we were somehow setting up the claims of human beings *against* the claims of God. Not at all: the claims of human beings *are* the claims of their Maker. There is no question of some kind of weighing to be done of the creature's dignity against that of the Creator. We are not between Scylla and Charybdis: divine majesty waiting to swallow us up and human presumption ready to suck us in. Our problem is not to steer between extremes nor to make a compromise. What we need is a kind of stereoscopic vision. The glory of God is both triumph and condescension, both action and passion. The dependent glory of humanity is both struggle and acceptance, both achievement and receptiveness. But it is easier to keep the pendulum swinging between opposites than to integrate those opposites.

FOR REFLECTION

Proverbs 18:32 (A.V.)

He that answereth a matter before he heareth it, it is folly and shame unto him.

H.H. Price, *Clarity is not enough*, Allen and Unwin 1963, p. 16

I should like to say at once that it will not do to put the complainants off with a merely "clever" rejoinder, which admits of no answer but produces no conviction. If the critics have not stated their own case properly (and I think that in some respects they have not) it is our business to state it better. If it appears to us that the demands which they make upon us are nonsensical as they stand, we must try to reformulate them in a way which does make sense. Then, but not before, we may express our disagreement with them.

David Jenkins, *What is man?* SCM Centrebooks 1970, pp. 14 and 15

Man is an object of endless fascination, concern, worry, enjoyment, despair, frustration and hope to himself. Past and present performance and history therefore suggest that men neither can nor will stop asking the question "What is man?". . . .

Thus, I am suggesting that it looks as if men have always asked "What is man?", that this is an odd fact about man itself, and that the question is an odd sort of question.

The Hope Of Heaven

Psalm 8

For I will consider thy heavens, even the works of thy fingers: the moon and stars, which thou hast ordained.

What is man, that thou art mindful of him: and the son of man, that thou visitest him?

Thou madest him lower than the angels: to crown him with glory and worship.

2

A Necessary End

Fearing death

Problems about human nature and destiny are threatening problems. We want reassurance. To ask about human durability is to plunge into human fears and hopes as well as to enquire about what is the case. Facts and values are intertwined. There are value questions about what we are worth and there is the bluntly factual question, Do we or do we not live on after death? Is death the end of us? We do not want it to be. The fear of death is as real as death itself and ought not to be repudiated as if it were irrelevant. It makes a logical and honest start to our questioning.

Shakespeare's Julius Caesar brushed the fear aside:

Of all the wonders that I yet have heard
It seems to me most strange that men should fear
Seeing that death, a necessary end
Will come when it will come.[1]

Perhaps that is a good attitude for a man who was going to be assassinated that day; but surely it is more human to identify with Claudio in *Measure for Measure*:

Ay, but to die, and go we know not where;
To lie in cold obstruction, and to rot;[2]

So he begs his sister to let him live, at the cost of her own virtue; and she dare not embark upon sympathizing with him: she has to be furious. All through the centuries human beings have tacitly

21

agreed that to admit to fearing death is dangerous, even treacherous, because it threatens to breach our flimsy defences.

Death is supposed to be defied or ignored, and in our times we are in an easier position for ignoring it through most of our lives than our ancestors ever were. Our expectation of life is much longer; most people die out of sight in hospital; when our leaders disgrace themselves there is no block on Tower Hill; people who have committed crimes, large or petty, no longer face the gallows; and the new thanksgiving service for the birth of a child has no need to lay emphasis on pre-servation from "the great danger of childbirth".

Yet still mortality is a hundred per cent; violence, intended by terrorists or unintended by road users, is very much with us; there remain plenty of killer dis-eases; premature death is as poignant as ever; the world is still a terrifying place; and sooner or later we have to reckon with finality. All these things hit us harder, not less hard, in the end, when we have not been brought up to face them in daily life.

For Christians, with the example of Christ at Gethsemane, to ignore death or even to defy it may well seem an odd response. We shall be more capable of responding fittingly in times of horror and dismay if first we can admit what we really feel: not in a panic, but in all seriousness. Perhaps there is help at hand if we ask for it. We are not likely to get the help we pretend not to need.

It is human to recognize how human Claudio's terror is. His earthly creator, we may say, has endowed him with the capacity for reactions which we can still share today. Yet times change even if human nature is con-stant, and if we are not bemused by splendid words we can realize that the substance of Claudio's fear of death is different from ours. Claudio takes some kind of life after death for granted but is terrified that it will be appalling. If Isabella had not been so angry in her own vulnerability, she might have comforted him with assurance of God's mercy.

Today we make no doubt that God will be merciful: on the contrary, we take His mercy for granted, if there is a God at all. Our feared alternative to life is not hell but nothingness. We worry that existence after death, far from being inevitable, is impossible. When life is good all the stoical philosophy in the world cannot make extinction anything but a disaster. If people think they do not mind it for themselves, they know they mind when they are confronted with the deaths of people they love. But, until quite recently, they have hardly been allowed to say so. Our "stiff upper lip" tradition, combined with the increasing normality of long life, have tended to make the arrival of death shocking in two senses, as trauma and also as embarrassment.

Looking for comfort

It is only fair to say that there has been a change lately for the better. Not the least achievement of the hospice movement has been to hasten this change, to thaw our frozen humanity and help not only cancer patients but the potential patients we all are to depend less upon evasions. Death has suddenly become so discussable as to be almost fashionable, a topic for little books and anthologies, a subject we can be taught about. The loneliness of fear is much mitigated.

In this as well as in medical ways the process of dying is being given real alleviation. People are indeed being enabled to live life to the full right to its end. In so far as it is true, as we are often told, that it is not after all death itself but the approach to it that makes people afraid, the compassionate wish to be a positive help to fellow human beings in their time of need is being granted today in remarkably full measure. But still, beyond the process of dying, there is death for the patient and bereavement for the patient's nearest and dearest. For all the care and all the honest discussion, the trauma of mortality of course remains.

So the embarrassment of helplessness recurs, making evasion still tempting and honesty still elusive. The human need for comfort is nothing to be ashamed of. Unfortunately it can be oddly inverted into a kind of duty for the miserable not to harrow other people's feelings, even to cheer up their sympathizers, or at least to accept comfort from them with reasonable alacrity.

There is usually some aspect of a situation which is less bad than it possibly might have been. "He didn't suffer"; or if clearly he did, "What a merciful release". So a cruel sort of obligation builds up for the survivors even to be grateful, rather than give way to grief and make everyone unhappy. Unfortunately this is the context in which the Christian hope is apt to be suddenly wheeled in, untried and unanalysed but desperately wanted. How can we not suspect in these circumstances that it is only facile wishful thinking?

For Christians to moralize and say "I told you so", or even, "Remember now thy Creator in the days of thy youth",[3] is not at all the point. Indeed there has been too much moralizing already. Faith seems to be something to be whipped up to order, and when it fails blame is added to sadness. Whether we have faith or lack it, or have a little faith which may or may not stand testing, we could do with a steady look at what faith promises.

Souls for survival?

Traditionally faithful people have felt assured that each of us has an immortal soul. It is no wonder that human beings have found this idea attractive. We know very well that our bodies die and that death is more drastic than sleep. It is not only philosophers who have taken hold of the idea that what dies is just an earthly envelope and our real selves are spiritual and imperishable. As far back as homo sapiens Neanderthalis, if serious burial of their dead is any indication, people seem to have begun to have some inkling, whether pious, terrified or hopeful, that there is "spirit" as well as body. To wonder and form opinions about a life beyond seems characteristic of human beings.

The idea of the soul as the true self has offered itself as a good, compact answer to certain persistent problems. The questions about our durability, our sacredness and our dangerous excellence seem to be answered all together. For many people assurance about souls underwrites their mortality. It provides a basis for their firm religious conviction that every single human life, however undeveloped, however damaged, is precious in the sight of God. The thought that each of us has an imperishable soul can encourage us to believe that unequal individual gifts do not matter ultimately because persons are to be respected *as* persons. So belief in "the soul" presents us with a hope of immortality, a way of understanding our value, and a reason for turning our backs on an earth-bound humanism. If only this belief were not itself so fraught with difficulties that it simply looks too good to be true!

Eternal souls brought in as a ready answer to mortality are apt to prove too flimsy to do the job. When "the soul" is produced as a sort of extra self with the role of carrying the immortality we hope for, we shall be faced, if anyone is unkind enough to press the questions, with fearful difficulties. What kind of thing can a "soul" be? Have we any real reason for thinking there is any such thing? How is it attached to the body

25

The Hope Of Heaven

while we live? What kind of life can it have on its own when its body has perished? Are we to expect our bodies to be gathered up and reconstituted, or will new ones be provided? If so, how will anyone know they are really ours?

Between the naïvety of some ideas of resurrection and the dreariness of simply becoming a ghost, we may well find that the more we ask these questions the less "wishful" our thinking becomes. We seem to be in a morass of dubious arguments to provide ourselves with immortal souls which we begin to wonder after all whether we really want. Doubts like this about the next world can even be reinforced by religious considerations. "Eternal life" cannot be a matter of mere survival. It must have something to do with a spiritual quality of life that at least begins here on earth. Perhaps we ought to be content with that and forget about the life hereafter? It could be salutary to remember that in early Israel there was no clear idea of heaven. It was in this world that God was to be known and served. Recently there have been impressive Christian thinkers who have firmly brought the meaning of "spiritual" back into this life. Such distinguished and diverse teachers as H.A. Williams[4] and D.Z. Phillips[5] rebuke any selfish or superstitious other-worldliness.

Yet ambiguity about our ultimate hope still seems, for a Christian, defeatist. "If for this life only we have hoped in Christ, we are of all men most to be pitied."[6] Must we really be expected to outgrow the question the Corinthians were asking: "How are the dead raised? With what kind of body do they come?"[7] On the contrary, if we are to hand on a recognizable Christian faith, we shall have to go on asking these questions.

Thinking about eternal rewards can be selfish, but putting them too firmly aside may not be very good for us either. Because heaven has been discounted, doing what we ought has come to the fore as if it were the whole substance of the Gospel. So virtue becomes its own reward with a vengeance. There is such a shyness today about affirming anything other-worldly that "religion" hardly seems to have much to do with eternal life at all. Sometimes Christianity even seems to be all about guilt: feeling guilty ourselves for not living up to Christian standards, and trying to make other people feel guilty too. There is plenty of guilt about. Some find most of it in private life and some in the life of society. But whatever the Kingdom of Heaven really is, it must be more than an appeal to our consciences. The Gospel has to do with what is going to happen to us and not only with what we ought to be doing or not doing. Dogged moralism can miss our deepest concerns as shortsightedly and unlovingly as neglectful carelessness.[8]

What we need is somehow to put Christian values and Christian beliefs properly together again. A Christian should be someone whose goodness and hopes are part of the same picture, not alternating with one another so that for years virtue tries to take over because hope seems unreal, and then in the end hope is brought out of retirement to counter despair. The final question about what really happens to us at death belongs with the other questions about the meaning of our existence. The life of the world to come cannot be produced at a moment's notice as a self-contained article of faith, but must have something to do with whatever we believe about human beings throughout their lives.

FOR REFLECTION

The Duc de Saint Simon, *Historical Memoirs II,
1710–1715* tr. Lucy Norton

For lack of other comfort I lived on my courage, telling
myself that one never experiences all the good or all
the evil that one has reason to expect.

William Cory (1823–1892), *Mimnermus in Church*

> You promise heavens free from strife,
>   Pure truth, and perfect change of will;
> But sweet, sweet is this human life,
>   So sweet, I fain would breathe it still;
> Your chilly stars I can forgo,
> This warm kind world is all I know.

Robert Browning, *Bishop Blougram's Apology*

> . . . Just when we are safest, there's a sunset-touch,
> A fancy from a flower-bell, someone's death,
> A chorus-ending from Euripides—
> And that's enough for fifty hopes and fears
> As old and new at once as nature's self,
> To rap and knock and enter in our soul,
> Take hands and dance there, a fantastic ring,
> Round the ancient idol, on his base again—
> The grand Perhaps:

A Necessary End

William Shakespeare, *Measure for Measure*, Act III Scene 1

Claudio   Ay, but to die, and go we know not where;
To lie in cold obstruction, and to rot;
This sensible warm motion to become
A kneaded clod; and the delighted spirit
To bathe in fiery floods or to reside
In thrilling region of thick-ribbed ice;
To be imprison'd in the viewless winds,
And blown with restless violence round about
The pendent world; or to be worse than worst
Of those that lawless and incertain thought
Imagine howling; 'tis too horrible.
The meanest and most loathed worldly life
That age, ache, penury, and imprisonment
Can lay on nature is a paradise
To what we fear of death.

Dame Cicely Saunders in *The Dictionary of Medical Ethics*

The focus of the modern hospice movement began with attention to the nature of terminal pain, to its better understanding and therefore more effective treatment. Alongside this came a revival of the old concept of "a good death" and attention to the achievements that a patient could still make in the face of physical deterioration . . .

3

Doubleness

Looking at people

In asking the questions we can hardly hope to eliminate wishful thinking entirely when our wishes are so much engaged; but we can take care which way we approach the problems. If we start with the seemingly simple enquiry "Have we souls?", we force the argument into a particular mould and invite everyone to take sides for or against "the soul". It is more promising to begin where we are and try to understand what we are. What is a human being? What is a person?

There is no need to ask for definitions or to make up our minds forthwith whether we will include Martians or angels or our favourite pets. We know at any rate that human beings, people, are our prime example of persons. There is something more that we know: people are embodied. So as soon as we start to think about persons as we find them, ourselves and other people, we have to take into account our physical natures. Christians are as well aware as their contemporaries that human beings are, at least, truly part of the material world. Whatever else we may be, we are a sort of animal and indeed, like the other animals, we are a sort of thing. The stuff of which we are made obeys biological, chemical and physical laws. We all die eventually and our bodies return to nature. There is no future in denying these facts, but we need to add to them another set of facts, equally obvious.

There is something about us which is not straightforwardly material, whether we call it consciousness, or reason, or go all the way and call it spirit. The most ardent materialist has to have some account to give of our tendency to picture ourselves as in some way *double*, physical and mental or material and spiritual: body and mind or body and soul. There is this characteristic and remarkable feature of human beings, and maybe of other creatures too, that they are "more than meets the eye", he, she or you rather than it, subjects rather than mere objects. The simplest way to see this is to imagine a surgeon operating on a brain. What is being cut up is cells not thoughts, even if a local anaesthetic is used and the patient is conscious: but the thoughts going on are as real in their mysterious way as the tissue that is being cut.

This doubleness, whatever it means, is not a comfortable way of life. We are not perfectly at home in the natural world, and if there is also a spiritual world we are certainly not perfectly at home in that. Many people are happy but nobody is perfectly happy, if only because we know that human life is transient.

It is no wonder that the ancient story that God fashioned Adam out of the dust of the earth and breathed into his nostrils the breath of life has made sense to so many generations. It picks out our continuity with nature and our evident distinctiveness. It is a picturesque way of announcing that human creatures are more than the stuff of which their bodies are formed. They are dust plus spirit, but "spirit" so far can be quite a commonsense notion. It is still in touch with its primary meaning, "breath". There is no need for it to take flight at once into metaphysics.

"The soul" in this elementary sense might not turn out to be either immortal or sacred; but there is something about a person which does lay a foundation for these ideas. People live with values, they look for meanings, and death comes as an enemy. If "the soul"

31

is wishful thinking, it is characteristic of us to have these wishful thoughts: they seem somehow to be natural to us.

Dualism

The most lofty theories have certainly been built upon this double character of human beings, and in particular the philosophical theory known as "dualism". Dualism is the belief that the essential part of a person is an immaterial soul, which may be associated with a body but which can also lead an independent existence. Presently it will need to be insisted that there is a great deal wrong with dualism as fully developed. But before being critical it is important to reiterate that this notion of body *and* spirit is not all theory but has a basis in everyday experience.

However doubtful we may be about souls, we cannot simply get rid of the whole idea. If we say that soul without body is merely ghost, we have to add that body without soul is merely corpse. While we are alive there is something about the sort of material object we call a human being that makes us more than *mere* material objects, and this is true even if one day we die for ever. There is more to human life, while it lasts, than dancing atoms or even growing cells.

In making *human* life so important we are still using it as the clearest example of this "doubleness". Animal rights enthusiasts can perfectly well point out that we are not as special as we like to think, and that plenty of animals have sensations and can suffer, and have their own skills and capacities. The "doubleness" of people as we know them, which commonsense picks on and philosophy builds on, is not something we have to be too possessive about. The point is that it does exist and we can find it in ourselves and the people around us. There really is such a being as a person, who as well as

32

an outward shape has something we can call an inner self.

The reason why dualism has been such a favourite theory is not merely that we want to believe in survival. Looking on ourselves and other people as somehow double beings is firmly built into our ordinary ways of thinking and speaking. "She could hardly keep body and soul together." "While I sit here in my armchair my thoughts fly through the whole universe." "The spirit is willing but the flesh is weak." "His mind has gone." "You will be with us in spirit." "In his big clumsy body was the spirit of a little child", or maybe, "of a mighty warrior." The idea has been ready to hand for poets:

> Her cabined ample spirit
> It fluttered and failed for breath.
> Tonight it doth inherit
> The vasty hall of death.[1]

When traditionalists who build a lot on the idea of the soul are accused of being falsely spiritual, they may retort that the recent fashion for emphasizing the "whole person" has not always been so obviously realistic. The ancient civil war between soul and body was not shadow-boxing, though it has been pacified by modern medicine and modern developments of hygiene. When these are removed the struggle is apt to renew itself, and the body once again takes on its role of rebellious enemy. When people travel as tourists to places where they find themselves vulnerable again to the major and minor inconveniences of prevalent infections, they may well begin to wonder whether some of our admirable new-found appreciation of our physical natures is a luxury of modern plumbing. At least they can reach a better understanding of all those fellow human beings, not so stupid after all, who have felt imprisoned in the body. How elevated one's thoughts could be, how one's spirit could soar, if only one did not feel so sick or poorly. That is not a "puritanical" way of thinking and has nothing to do with disapproving of the body or stopping anybody's healthy enjoyment. It is a matter of wanting to be set free into greater, not less, capability. St Bernard of Clairvaux said, "Leave your bodies outside. Here only souls enter", and to us this normally sounds like a gloomy threat. One can come to see that it could have been a promise. The notion of human beings as half beasts, half angels was not altogether perverse but had a kind of realism about it. It has tended to fit a good many of the facts of human experience.

Even "evidence for survival" is not entirely negligible. People who brush it aside unexamined risk being as unscientific as people who glory in it. Christians are deeply suspicious of paranormal phenomena, except for their own miracles, but there are after all some curious unexplained facts: not conclusive but interesting. People have claimed to communicate with the dead, and generally seem to be going a long way beyond the evidence; but some of the data seem hard to explain without the hypothesis of telepathy between the living. But if telepathy is possible, then materialism is false. This is not so much an argument *for* survival as a big breach in the argument *against* it.[2]

Likewise people at the point of death have described experiences "out of the body", experiences which seem to confirm a dualistic belief in the soul. It must be said again and again that there is no proof of survival here. To have almost died is *not* to have returned from death. But once again what the evidence does is make a hole in materialism. It is fair to argue that if a single such case "actually happens, then mind and body are separable, and the death of the body does not imply the death of the mind".[3] The debate goes on.

"Why, of old", said Browning's Mr Sludge, "the
  medium",
"Great men spent years and years in writing books
To prove we've souls, and hardly proved it then."

Lonely souls

Why then should a Christian not leap on to "dualism"
and ride it like a lively and well-trained horse on which
to canter cheerfully into the next world? Unfortunately
it is too big a jump from commonsense "doubleness" or
even from extra-sensory perception to immortal souls.
Even though we are more than our bodies, we have not
yet been offered any assurance that we can outlast
them. It is time to state bluntly that dualism as a
theory lets us down, and that Christians need not be
too anxious to hang on to this one particular view of
what people really are.

Indeed dualism is a dangerous friend for Christian
theology. Far from establishing our future hope, it sets
up enormous difficulties in understanding our present
existence. The way of theorizing about our
"doubleness" which was inaugurated by Descartes in
the seventeenth century has a good deal to answer for.
It has hardened into an unsatisfactory tradition for
both philosophers and theologians, encouraging them
to take body and soul apart when they are hardly
capable of putting them together again.

According to dualism, souls are "immaterial sub-
stances" which are beings in their own right. So the
connection of these souls with the bodies that somehow
belong to them becomes not just interestingly mysterious but bafflingly obscure; and their presumed
re-connection eventually to resurrection bodies is no
clearer. Since Descartes put philosophy on this track,
thousands of pages of fascinating but inconclusive discussion have been written on "the mind-body problem",

"survival", "personal identity". It is only fair to point out that Descartes himself did not think of the soul as lodged in the body like a pilot in a vessel.[4] On the contrary, he insisted that it is not. But he did emphasize that "body" and "consciousness" are different kinds of thing. As he put it, bodies are "extended", that is, take up space, whereas the soul is characterized by *thinking*.[5]

With hindsight we can see that this beautifully clear distinction already begins to nudge commonsense out of the way by quietly making the real self the thinking self. The trouble with the tradition Descartes founded is that it became obsessed with the problem of how we know anything. Descartes in his integrity gave so much weight to the question "How can I know?" that his legacy has been to detach the person, as thinker, from the real live world and enclose him in his own thoughts. Descartes' famous answer, "I think, therefore I am", basing everything – God, oneself, other people, the world – on this one thing one cannot doubt, that there is a doubter,[6] converts the soul into the mind, and then removes it from everyday life into a world of its own. Having walked into this philosophical lobster pot one can hardly get out of it. The idea that is supposed to set us free shuts us up in our own selves, cut off from the things and people we know perfectly well in real life by layers of doubt and scepticism which have to be elaborately dealt with once we have begun on this line of thought at all. Far from being assured of another life, a soul like this could seem to lose its grip on this life.

The tradition in British philosophy is to put more weight on experience and less on unaided reason when challenged to say how we know anything. But unfortunately the appeal to experience, down-to-earth as it sounds, can also lead to a sceptical dead-end. For how do I know that you have the same experiences as I do?

Are we using words to mean something quite different? We are as much shut up in our own worlds as ever. It is Hume the robust sceptic not Berkeley the brilliant bishop who is the culmination of the school of thought called "the British empiricists". Hume, in a sort of mischievous rather than malicious spirit, even reduced the person to a mere bundle of experiences and could only recommend "carelessness and inattention"[7] as a way of letting commonsense reassert itself.

The trouble is that once I have taken up the position of the lone doubter, there seems to be a gap between me on the one hand with my thoughts and experiences, and the real world somewhere out there which can presumably send me messages but which I can never get at directly. The harder philosophers try to bridge this gap between myself and reality, the more they seem to find a gap to bridge. "Myself" is a good English word, but with very little encouragement philosophers begin to discuss my self and then "selves".[8] So, whether by reason or experience, they arrive by easy stages at a picture of a world where a person is primarily a dis-embodied consciousness, a mind, a self-contained thinker of thoughts or a passive receiving set for ex-periences cut off from all the other "selves" there may happen to be. "Selves" can never be really sure whether they truly are in touch with one another or whether they are living in a dream world. They have problems: "other minds", "perception", "personal identity". Are there any other people? Are material things real? Am I two beings, a mind and a body? These were live questions when philosophers took stock of their posi-tion just after the Second World War, and it took a revolution in philosophy to get out of the trap.

Christians have found it quite as difficult as other thinkers to extricate themselves from the problems of dualism and return to a commonsense understanding of the fundamental wholeness of the person. They have had a loyalty to the idea of the soul as a detachable being. They have feared with some reason that without dualism our spiritual natures might be taken away from us, and our real doubleness disappear into materialism. So Christians may seem to love the problems and not want them answered. They rather like the idea that only God can guarantee our knowledge of the world and one another. They have given the impression of commitment to a kind of mirror image of materialism which might be called "soul-ism", the idea that the thinking soul is the only important part of us. This is a strange notion for Christians, who proclaim a somewhat materialist faith in a God who lived and died and rose again in human flesh, and communicates with His people by sacraments. It has been left to secular and even sceptical philosophers to realize that dualism was making people into "ghosts in machines".

FOR REFLECTION

Plato *Apology*

Socrates: Above all, I shall then be able to continue my search into true and false knowledge; as in this world, so also in the next; and I shall find out who is wise, and who pretends to be wise, and is not. What would not a man give, O judges, to be able to examine the leader of the great Trojan expedition; or Odysseus or Sisyphus, or numberless others, men and women too! What infinite delight would there be in conversing with them and asking them questions! In another world they do not put a man to death for asking questions: assuredly not. For besides being happier than we are, they will be immortal, if what is said is true.

Phaedo

We will do our best, said Crito: And in what way shall we bury you?

In any way that you like; but you must get hold of me, and take care that I do not run away from you.

Descartes, *Meditations* (in *Body, Mind and Death*, ed. A. Flew, p. 132)

I am, however, a real thing and really exist; but what thing? I have answered: a thing which thinks.

Stuart Hampshire, *Mind* 1950, p. 239

So far from being imposed on the plain man by philosophical theorists, and even less by seventeenth-century theorists, the myth of the mind as a ghost within the body is one of the most primitive and natural of all the innumerable myths which are deeply imbedded in the vocabulary and structure of our languages. The plain fact is that in many (perhaps most) European languages the words for mind, soul or spirit are the same as, or have the same roots as, the words for ghost, and were the same long before Descartes or modern mechanics were conceived.

C.A. Mace "The 'Body-Mind Problem' in Philosophy, Psychology and Medicine", *Philosophy* 1966, p. 154

Large hypotheses are very rarely refuted outright. What more often happens is that a theory encounters difficulties. These difficulties pile up and people *get exasperated* by them, or they just get tired of the hypothesis and become disposed to try another line of thought.

Anthony Flew, *Body, Mind and Death* (Introduction), p.12

People are what you meet.

Bernard Williams, "Personal identity and individuation" in *Essays in Philosophical Psychology*, Macmillan 1967, ed. D.F. Gustafson, p.337

Suppose a magician is hired to perform the old trick of making the emperor and the peasant become each other. He gets the emperor and the peasant in one room, with the emperor on his throne and the peasant in the corner, and then casts the spell. What will count as success? Clearly not that after the smoke has cleared the old emperor should be in the corner and the old peasant on the throne. That would be a rather boring trick. The requirement is presumably that the emperor's body, with the peasant's personality, should be on the throne, and the peasant's body, with the emperor's personality, in the corner. What does this mean? In particular, what has happened to the voices? The voice presumably ought to count as a bodily function; yet how would the peasant's gruff blasphemies be uttered in the emperor's cultivated tones, or the emperor's witticisms in the peasant's growl? A similar point holds for the features; the emperor's body might include the sort of face that just *could not* express the peasant's morose suspiciousness, the peasant's a face no expression of which could be taken for one of fastidious arrogance.

4

Wholeness

The ghost in the machine

Christians have no wish to be intellectual snobs. They know perfectly well that a "soul" is not just a clever mind. But they do want to reject materialism, and this is apt to mean that the body is put on one side and everything else on the other. People who think that religious faith requires them to be dualists are under strong pressure to use "soul", "mind", "consciousness", "self" almost interchangeably to mean the real person in contrast to the mere body.

It was Gilbert Ryle who brilliantly caricatured all this as "the dogma of the Ghost in the Machine". His book *The Concept of Mind* was the most vivid, comprehensible and effective working out of the philosophical revolution which took its rise from Wittgenstein. Ryle was not exactly a materialist. He was not denying that we are more than our bodies. He was denying that the "more" consists of extra little intellectual people inside us. He was not trying to do away with our inner lives but to make more sense of them. Mind and body make one person, living in one real accessible world. There is not one thing, called the mind, that does the thinking and another thing, called the body, that does the walking.

Looking for minds as separate hidden entities somehow associated with bodies is, according to Ryle, a "category mistake": the same kind of mistake as watching the bowling, the batting and the fielding in cricket and then asking when we are going to see the team spirit. To say that we are made up of mind and body ought to be a kind of joke like "She came home in a sedan chair and a flood of tears".[1] Complaining that I cannot see your mind is a little like complaining that I have never seen an "average family" with two and a half children. Consciousness is real enough but Ryle maintained that since Descartes we had got into the habit of talking about consciousness in muddling ways.

So when we do something thoughtfully we are not performing two actions at once, moving our limbs and also keeping up a running commentary of secret thoughts. Intelligent actions are all of a piece, not split. Of course we are capable of keeping our thoughts secret. We can be reticent or even hypocritical, but that is quite sophisticated. Openness is primary. Knowing ourselves is not having "privileged access" to a private screen-show, and knowing other people is not chancy guesswork. "In making sense of what you say, in appreciating your jokes, in unmasking your chess-stratagems, in following your arguments and in hearing you pick holes in my arguments, I am not inferring to the workings of your mind, I am following them."[2]

Ryle wrote "with deliberate abusiveness".[3] His polemics, he assured his readers, were mainly to clear away assumptions of which he himself had been a victim. No doubt he overstated the case and cleared away too much of the mystery of the human soul. But what his fresh approach did, with commonsense and vigour and clarity, was let us be in touch again with one another and with things we can see and feel. We are not isolated "selves" but people, in communication with each other all along. Often we are doubtful about all sorts of things, but our doubts are secondary to our certainties. Philosophical scepticism is not some kind of intellectual duty but an aberration.

Commonsense is not everything. Christians are naturally pleased that, since *The Concept of Mind* was written, mystery and even metaphysics have edged their way back into philosophical respectability. But nor is metaphysics everything. Christians ought not to put metaphysics first and commonsense second. The firm reality of the creation ought to mean more to them than the theories to which it gives rise. They have every reason to be grateful to the philosophers who allowed human life as we find it to be presentable again and encouraged us to pay attention to ordinary language.

One world

In *The Concept of Mind* Ryle set about abolishing old errors. He made it impossible for people who want philosophers to attend to them to talk in certain ways any more. What is not so well known is that the upshot can be positive not negative. To be set free from dualism is to be given a better chance of doing justice to the unity of the person.

The ghost in the machine has had a better run for its money than it deserves because it has seemed to be our only defender against materialism. Our fear is that without the ghost there will be only the machine, so that we shall have to say that people just are their bodies. If we cannot believe that is the whole truth, it is worth taking a little trouble to see what to say instead. Dualism is not the only way of reckoning with the "doubleness" of a human being. Instead of taking the whole person apart as dualism does, or denying the doubleness as materialism does, we can begin with the unity and then allow for the doubleness.

For this *The Concept of Mind* sets us free. Since the drubbing it gave to the ghost, we have been made to look for some other account of a human being than an immaterial spirit residing in a body. We can see that it is a counsel of despair to say that there are minds and there are bodies, and heaven knows how they are joined. What we need to say is that anyway we know that there are people. Then we can take ghosts and corpses as derivative ideas, which we should never have needed to think about unless we had first known what a person is. Our doubleness is secondary to our wholeness. A person is not two beings, one conscious, the other physical. We have after all come across enough people to recognize what they are. A person just is this double kind of being. Professor P.F. Strawson argued this out with great stringency in his book *Individuals*. It is the *same* individual who weighs ten stone, is thinking hard, and believes in God, not two individuals mysteriously united.[4]

Yet surely bodies and souls are still distinct notions? By all means: something can be derivative without being unreal. This is a matter of organizing our ideas, not of denying any of them. We can talk as much as we find convenient about bodies and souls, once we stop mistaking either of them for complete people. It is when we try to take them apart too soon that the difficulties of dualism make themselves felt.

The trouble with the immaterial soul as the real person is quite simple: we cannot find it. In a way this is no more than a platitude. The ordinary meaning of "to find" just is to get into a position where we can see, or touch, or hear, or smell what we are hunting for. We cannot play hunt the thimble with an invisible thimble. Other ways of talking about finding and seeing depend on the basic meaning. Sometimes we talk in metaphors and say we "see" something like the answer to an abstract problem; but we should never put it that way unless generally people saw with their eyes. When people report sightings of a ghost they describe a being with some kind of palpable body, perhaps with a beard that is "a sable silvered". If they say, "I saw nothing, heard nothing, felt nothing", we know that the ghost has not appeared this time. If it never appears we soon become rather sceptical about it. Living people identify one another and get in touch with one another in various ways, all of which presuppose that the world we live in is physical. Christians will not be listened to when they talk of the presence of God and of another life in which we shall see Him unless they can come to terms with the basic physical meaning of "presence".

People as doers

Neither ghost nor machine can stand in for the whole person, and there is no way of sticking these incompatible components together. They have to be united not just joined. The clue we need is the idea of *activity*, which brings "soul" and "body" together into one person, because it shows what "body" has to do with "soul". To be alive is to be in some sort of two-way relationship with an outside reality. Consciousness on its own would be literally "out of touch". We do not sit inside our heads looking out through our eyes: we *do* things. The soul as an "immaterial substance" is too refined to be a real person. Hands and feet are not tools that our minds somehow learn to use: they are part of ourselves. Looking without handling is sophisticated. To be in touch is where we start, not a goal we may reach if we are clever enough.

One sort of activity is cogitating. Rodin's "Thinker", who sits and thinks, is not the basic human being: he is a specialist. Thinking is what he is doing: he is not thinking apart from doing. If we were all thinkers first and had to become doers, it is hard to see how we could ever begin to get any purchase on the outside world.

On the contrary, human beings are practical creatures from their origins. Our earliest ancestors did not first develop their big brains and then, as "rational animals", begin to use them. Body, mind and what we want to call spirit seem to have evolved all of a piece. Long before homo sapiens there came homo habilis, whose clever hands made tools. It would be odd if what we can find out about our origins did not make philosophical sense, as if "the soul" meant "a thinking thing" by the time Descartes began to puzzle about it, whereas in the days when Cro-Magnon man emerged "the soul" meant something much more practical.

Not only for homo sapiens as a species but also for each of us as an individual, it makes sense to look at the reality of human development: and dualism still shows up poorly. Only fear of materialism could make it seem satisfactory to imagine each human soul as an isolated consciousness, needing to work out that there are other people in the world and wanting arguments to go on believing this. Nobody who has dealings with babies is likely to see them as rational spirits newly endowed with bodies, embarking on a process of getting in touch with the rest of us. Nursery "solipsism" is nonsense. On the contrary, it is separate independence which needs to be learnt, both physical and mental. We are taught to feed ourselves and to think for ourselves, and one world in which we already belong is presupposed. To ask how we know it is real is like asking how the child is assured that its mother is real. Human beings start at home in the world of people and things. To explore, even to lose touch, or perhaps to withdraw into oneself, may come later. Interconnectedness with people and things, in widening circles, is more fundamental to a new member of humankind than the self-awareness that characterizes a mature person. We learn by doing, we live by doing.

Theologians ought to be concerned as much as philosophers with the idea of the person as one and the person as active: and so indeed they have been. The

47

emphasis on activity has been, not "trendy", but a strong and wholesome trend among diverse thinkers during the last forty years. It is activity, not merely thinking nor merely feeling, which constitutes a person. People are active and interactive, and the "mental" is not to be put in a separate compartment from the material world in which we are embodied. The physical creation of which we take ourselves to be a part is not a confidence trick. No doubt there is more to it than meets the eye, but we can safely start with what does meet the eye. The three-dimensional lives we think we live are real.

Keeping in touch

Practical activity looks more like the reality of human life than immaterial souls in their rational isolation. The important fact which is beginning to emerge is that being a person has something fundamental to do with communication. To spell out what this means, including what it means for the Christian faith, can eventually provide us with a more realiable hope than dualism. The longer way round after all may turn out to be the shorter way home.

Communicating is not something that a person just happens to do and might not do. We deny that a being is a person at all if there is no question of its getting into communication with anyone. A tree is not a person. Nor is an amoeba. A dog might be, in a way. A child is a person. A foetus is on the way to being one. Inhabitants of other worlds might read our radio signals. A dead man can never communicate any more; or can he? That is what we really want to know when we ask whether he has a soul. When religious people talk about a personal God, it is because they believe that in some way they have heard His word.

Our capacity to communicate makes us what we are.

Wholeness

Human beings, like other animals, have many characteristic abilities which make life worthwhile. We have no wings to fly with, but we have eyes and ears, hands and feet and voices. We expect to be able to see and hear, walk and speak. A good many of us can read and write and calculate, and some of us can sing. To be deprived of these capabilities is to be handicapped, maybe grievously. But to be unable to communicate is something worse. It is a fundamental deprivation. That is why even mild autism is such a problem. Solitary confinement and paralyzing strokes are terrible because they attack the basis of humanity. People who overcome them do so by recovering their powers of communication as best they may, not by developing other powers instead. They find ways of gaining access to the written word, they convey messages in ingenious ways, they exercise their minds and muscles to keep in touch somehow with other people. The threat they are faced with is to become the isolated selves that dualism would have us all to be.

FOR REFLECTION

Stuart Hampshire, *Thought and Action*, Chatto and Windus 1959, p.53

We are in the world, as bodies among bodies, not only as observers but as active experimenters.

Ian Ramsey, Bishop of Durham, "The Theology of Wholeness" in *From Fear to Faith*, ed. Norman Autton, SPCK 1971, p.82

What this means is that concepts such as body and mind, body and soul are to be subsumed under the concept of person, that activity which informs our very being, that which makes each of us himself or herself.

John Pobee, *Towards an African Theology*, Abingdon 1979, p.49

Whereas Descartes spoke for Western man when he said *cogito ergo sum* – I think, therefore I exist – Akan man's ontology is *cognatus ergo sum* – I am related by blood, therefore I exist, or I exist because I belong to a family. And a family, which is the basic unit, consists of the living, the dead, and the yet-to-be-born.

Wholeness

Robert Browning, "Fra Lippo Lippi"

. . .
Or say there's beauty with no soul at all –
(I never saw it – put the case the same –)
If you get simple beauty and nought else,
You get about the best thing God invents:
That's somewhat: and you'll find the soul
    you have missed,
Within yourself, when you return him thanks.

5

Embodiment

Rational animals?

One reason why people have written off the body so easily, and over-spiritualized their hopes, is that they have been used to think of the body as only what we have in common with all the other animals. We consider the beasts which perish, and as far as the body is concerned we are on a level with them. Our bodies are mortal like theirs. We rise above the beasts by our "reason": so surely it has to be our reason that is the basis of our "souls"?

It is not hard to persuade people who spend their lives trying to be rational that it is the thinking part of us which both deserves to be immortal and is likely to be so. Reason may not be the whole person, but at least it is deemed to be the superior part of the human being. So when the body dies the soul in its capacity of "mind" is all set to take over and keep us going, at least to bridge the gap between this world and the next.

But alongside this conviction of superiority has gone a too limited notion of reason as something austerely mental and individual, belonging to each *man* as all alone he confronted his Maker. Women were not meant to be excluded, but this way of putting the case has let them be readily overlooked, not quite rational, not quite human. Likewise people whose strength or skill is physical not intellectual were not meant to be patronized; but still it has come easily to scholars to think of abstract reflection as more fully human than physical exertion, and calm contemplation as more creditable than emotion.

Embodiment

No wonder there is a reaction going on against the overweening intellect: a reaction which is all to the good as long as it is in the name of the whole person, not just a new tyranny of "heart" over "head" instead of "head" over "heart". We may be glad that rational people are being encouraged again to have feelings and to show them. The "stiff upper lip" is going out of fashion, and even grown men may be allowed to cry. The senses are coming into their own as an honourable part of our humanity.

If the recovery of emphasis upon the physical is to be a benefit rather than an embarrassment we need *tact*, "the faculty of saying or doing the right thing at the right time"; and tact itself is rooted in the physical notions of "keeping in touch" and of "getting the feel of things". There are many such reminders built into our language that bodies represent sensitivity as well as sensuality. Even at our most intellectual, we *see* connections and *grasp* the truth.

But then are we to write off the characteristic rationality which we have been brought up to think of as the glory of our species? Are we no more than one sort of animal who has specialized in ratiocination? We do sums, but birds build nests, which is just as difficult. Like most correctives this one can easily go too far. We may start belittling human beings instead of appreciating other creatures better. If we stop looking on reason as the godlike and immortal part of us, we may begin to think of ourselves merely as clever destructive little beasts, more trouble than we are worth. "Reason" becomes an embarrassment. We feel we have to apologize for it as "mere rationality". If our large brains distinguish us from the other animals, they allow us to be more dangerous, not more splendid.

Since we dare not say that humanity qualifies for eternal life by passing an intelligence test, the risk is that we shall go to the other extreme and lose our

wonder at the marvellous creature a human being is.
"What a piece of work is a man!" said Hamlet,[1] "How
noble in reason! How infinite in faculty! in form, in
moving, how express and admirable! in action how like
an angel! in apprehension how like a god! the beauty of
the world! the paragon of animals!" Surely it is not just
arrogance to warm to this and be unwilling to go all the
way with Hamlet's conclusion "And yet, to me, what is
this quintessence of dust?"

There is a way to go on marvelling at the glory of
humanity without cutting ourselves off from our roots
in the physical creation: a way which finds our real
distinctive rationality in our capacity to use language
for communication. What we need to do is link reason
firmly, as the Greeks did, to the idea of the *word*.

English-speaking Christians who read com-
mentaries have come across this link between "word"
and "reason" in one particular context. In the Prologue
to the Fourth Gospel, *logos* ought to mean both, and
our translators have had to select one. They have
chosen to say that "In the beginning was the word", but
have hastened to explain that this does not capture the
whole meaning. God's *Word* made flesh was also the
Reason behind the universe. Nothing less than this,
the Fourth Gospel tells us, was brought to earth to
dwell among us in Jesus of Nazareth.

It would be a pity to be so elevated by the theology as
to suppose that reason and word belong together only
when we are talking about God. Our human
rationality has almost everything to do with our
capacity to shape our thoughts in language. Poetically
Edwin Muir distinguished mankind from the animals,
who live wholly in the present:

> No word do they have, not one
> To plant a foot upon . . .
> For with names the world was called
> Out of the empty air . . .[2]

More prosaically the philosopher H.H. Price used to say the same thing, that "thinking in absence" is made possible for human beings by the use of symbols. Plenty of animals can communicate effectively with one another, and some of them can understand words of ours, but they have not made this great breakthrough. It is not just that they lack vocalization. Wittgenstein put it negatively: "*The limits of my language* mean the limits of my world".[3] Positively, we can see how it is language that stretches our universe for us beyond the immediate present, and opens up for human creatures whole worlds of reality and of imagination which make them almost as gods. God's Word is spirit and has become flesh. Our words are flesh: they start as physical, whether they are spoken or written, but they seem to become spirit. Using them and understanding them raises us above our merely physical surroundings.

However deprecating we may want to be about the pretensions of mankind, there is something wonderful here which demands acknowledgement. Beyond any parochial affection for our own species, and certainly beyond any cold intellectualism, there is after all a suitable kind of admiration for what reason signifies for humanity. It is right to look at the "rational animal" with a kind of hopeful reverence. The less acceptable face of rationality needs to be fairly regarded, but not without appreciation for the marvellous achievement, or gift, of articulate thought. But if we locate our characteristic humanity here, we have by no means separated it from our brains and tongues and ears.

Ghosts need machines

Before Christians can cheerfully adopt this way of regarding a human being as a whole they may need a good deal more reassurance. It still seems to have a suspicious flavour of materialism hanging about it, a lack of interest in any other world but this. The philosophers who have been most concerned to get rid of the ghost in the machine have not been religiously inclined. They have not really minded getting rid of souls altogether while they were about it. Many of us are not able to be so disinterested. We cannot help letting our minds wander to the question of what is going to become of us. The whole person is all very well in this world, but does it give us any hope for the next? We cannot get away from the fact that the body does perish. If I live as a whole, how can I expect not to die as a whole?

Christians have uttered the answer many times in reciting the Creeds. They believe in the resurrection of the body. We live as a whole, die as a whole, *and* are raised as a whole. But it has been too easy to jump to the conclusion that this would have to mean the gathering up somehow of our mortal flesh from all over the place, from earth and ashes and other creatures' digestions. No wonder Christians today put the idea of resurrection away in the back of their minds as crude and naïve. The immortal soul that survives the body whatever happens, keeps presenting itself as a more attractive option. Try as we may to look at people as wholes, the ghost in the machine goes on haunting us, too welcome a visitant to be quickly exorcized.

So it looks like a short cut to hope to let souls and bodies be taken apart. Dualism appeals to genuine and honourable longings, it offers an attractive explanation of real facts, and so it lures us to overlook its essential wrongheadedness. What is wrong with it is the persistent assumption that the real "I" is a spirit camping out in a body. It is only too clear that the human frame is not able to support us at the standard to which we are accustomed for much more than its understood three score years and ten or fourscore years, so no wonder we ask whether "we" can carry on without it.

Even to put the question in that way handicaps us in trying to answer it. The moment we have granted that our bodies let "us" down we have separated the physical body from the "real self". Are hands and feet and eyes and mouths, even hearts and brains, only something we *have*, not part of the real "us" at all? By making our bodies seem like an optional extra we have as it were disembodied ourselves without first finding out what embodiment means.

People who think "the soul" is just nonsense beg the question the other way. It takes somebody who is prepared to think about survival and consider what it would involve to explain why bodies are not just like clothes, something we can take off. What we need to do to see the point is imagine, not just in general but in detail, what it would be like to be disembodied.[4] We may have accepted the idea that spirits are hard to find, and yet assumed that it would be perfectly all right to *be* a spirit. But suppose I am a ghost returned to my old home with a message for the people who are living there now? How am I to get in touch with them? If I have no body I must be invisible and voiceless. There is my desk and a pen lying on it, but I cannot pick it up and write as I have no hands. Worse, how can I even see it, as I have no eyes? If we imagine that ghosts can easily tap tables or throw the furniture about, we have not seriously asked the question, how? We think of them with faint bodies like ghosts in films. We need to face the fact that beings without bodies have no way of doing things or of having things done to them. There is not much they can do even on their own. Can they move about from one place to another? Can they listen to other people's conversations, or to music? The trouble is that without ears to pick up particular sound waves it is impossible to say which sounds a disembodied person would hear.

The Hope Of Heaven

Disembodiment would be a kind of extreme case of imprisonment or paralysis, the total unavailability of one's body. People whose belief in immortal souls comes easily imagine getting out of their bodies like getting out of prison. On the contrary, our freedom to live and act, rightly understood, has to be the full possession of physical powers. We may well ask, How are the dead raised and with what *body* do they come?[5] In other words, how are they going to communicate with one another? To get in touch with a disembodied person must be more difficult than meeting a stranger at a busy railway station. We may well hope for a new heaven and a new earth where Christian love will be put into practice; but any heaven and earth in which numbers of people are to live must fill the role the material world fills now, of keeping us in touch.

It is no use supposing, for instance, that human affection is something we could simply carry on if we were bodiless spirits. We look at our friends, listen to them, smile at them, speak to them, write them letters. Even the telephone, disembodied voice as it is, conveys sound waves by way of electrical impulses. Unless we have eyes or ears, tongues or fingers we cannot establish communication with anyone. Telepathy might be an exception, but if it were the only kind of communication we had it is hard to see how we could tell what was a telepathic message and what was our own imagining; and in any case telepathy would have to be about something. It would not make us independent of an outside world of real bodies.

So a completely disembodied person is a ghost without a machine, helplessly inactive. He can only live in his memories or maybe take some kind of interest in human affairs without being able to join in. After a while his individuality is bound to fade away. So, as Professor Strawson put it "Disembodied survival, on such terms as these, may well seem unattractive. No doubt it is for this reason that the orthodox have wisely insisted on the resurrection of the body."[6]

Of course this is ironical, but it ought not to make Christians too anxious. They have after all heard something like it before. "Here indeed we groan, and long to put on our heavenly dwelling,so that by putting it on we may not be found naked."[7] One interpretation of this is that St Paul feared the "nakedness" of the soul for reasons not very different from those given by Professor Strawson. The disembodied soul is, literally, out of touch.

What philosophers are now emphasizing, plenty of unphilosophical people, including some religious ones, have known all along. Alongside noble aspiration about immortality there have always been less happy expectations. "The dead praise not Thee, O Lord: neither all they that go down into silence."[8] Survival has been pictured, without wishful thinking, as a shadowy half existence in a dreary. underworld. Homer's dead people have to drink blood before they can speak to Odysseus. His mother explains why she cannot embrace him: "You are only witnessing here the law of our mortal nature, when we come to die. We no longer have sinews keeping the bones and flesh together."[9] Likewise Achilles would rather be a serf among the living than king among the dead. Unless we may hope for resurrection of the whole person, we have little ground for assuming that immortality as such must be uplifting.

FOR REFLECTION

Mary Midgley, *Beast and Man: The Roots of Human Nature*, Harvester 1978, p. 335

. . . If we are to compare the basic elements of human social life with those of any other species, we need to use analogies, because many of the functions these elements serve simply are not served in any other primate species. Primates do not have big co-operative enterprises, nor therefore the loyalty, fidelity, and developed skills that go with them. Nor do they have fixed homes and families. But the hunting carnivores do. And neither apes nor wolves have anything like the human length of life, nor therefore the same chance of accumulating wisdom and of deepening relationships. But elephants do. And no mammal really shares the strong visual interest that is so important both to our social life and to our art, nor perhaps needs to work as hard as we do to rear our young. But birds do. This is why it is vacuous to talk of "the difference between man and animal" without saying *which* animal.

Hosea 14:2
Take with you words, and turn to the Lord.

P.F. Strawson, *Individuals*, Methuen 1959, p. 116
. . . the strictly disembodied individual is strictly solitary.

6

Presence

Where is God?

This emphasis on the physical world is not "materialism". Materialism is the dogma that there is only the physical world. To a real materialist, "spirit" is simply an idea with no sense, and people after all just are their bodies. What we are saying is that spirit needs body.

But then a great difficulty looms up, which is apt to give religious people the feeling that we should go back to dualism. To insist on whole persons is all very well for human beings. To utter the most lofty thoughts we need vocal cords, or hands to write with, or some way of signalling that other people can receive. But what about God? God is spirit. God has to be disembodied. So when we cast doubt on the notion of effective disembodiment what we are running into is not materialism but worse, atheism. Is God a ghost without a machine? It is no wonder that people have such difficulty in finding Him. It seems that we can never grasp Him, literally or metaphorically. Is He a person at all, since persons need bodies to communicate with one another? It begins to look as if God is nowhere. Perhaps He is nothing. Are we to take refuge in mystery and say "Well, it just is beyond our understanding"? Some people think they understand only too well that we have reached a contradiction.[1]

What may help is to take seriously the idea that God is not nowhere, but everywhere. He is infinitely present, not infinitely absent. He is not disembodied in any negative sense. There is no body which is not His body. That sounds like "pantheism" and Christians take fright. We are not allowed to say that God *is* the universe or that the universe *is* God. If we suggest anything of the kind we are falling into idolatry or nonsense or both. But some Christian thinkers lately have taken hold of another technical term, "pan-entheism", "all-in-God-ism", offered as a way of responsibly relating God to everything there is.[2]

God is much more than the physical universe but there is no need to think of Him as *dis*embodied. As Creator and Upholder of all things He is totally "in touch" with everything. He knows what is happening everywhere more directly than we know what is happening in our own bodies. We are both powerful, and vulnerable, through our separate bodies; and we may imagine that God is powerful, and vulnerable, through every creature. Not a sparrow falls without His presence.[3] "Raise the stone and you shall find me: cleave the wood and I am there."[4] This notion is as mysterious as anyone could wish, but it is not a blank mystery which we fall back upon after losing an argument. Indeed this way of thinking has been a lively part of our religious tradition. "The word is very near you; it is in your mouth and in your heart."[5] "He is not far from each one of us, for 'In him we live and move and have our being'."[6] This is no new fangled twentieth-century notion brought in to help us out of a difficulty. It comes from the account of Paul's speech at Athens, presented as common ground between Paul and the Gentiles he hoped to convert.

Christians need not stop short at saying that God is everywhere. They also characteristically affirm that He is in particular places. He has many ways of making Himself present to people. Above all, He was present in one human being. We say that God was embodied in Jesus of Nazareth. Does that not give Him body enough? It does, but only for people who already have some notion what they are talking about when they speak of God's presence. There has to be a Word to be made flesh. As the Epistle to the Hebrews put it, "In many and various ways God spoke of old to our fathers by the prophets; but in these last days he has spoken to us by a Son."[7] God appeared to Moses in the burning bush,[8] and to Isaiah in the Temple.[9] These great manifestations are backed up by countless people's conviction, all down the centuries, that in their own way they too have been aware of God's presence. When we ask them how, they will often speak of scriptures or of sacraments, understood as pledges of His presence. To believe in a personal God is to believe in an ultimately findable God.

But still God does not have to be easy to find. He can choose when and where He will be present. He can hide and seem to be absent. "We stand before God and we shout into an empty sky, out of which there is no reply", said Metropolitan Anthony Bloom at the beginning of one of his books.[10] If we could just walk into God's presence, He would be an idol. There is nowhere that He cannot be, and nowhere that we can catch Him and make Him stop. Human beings cannot contain God in the houses they build with hands: but they can invite Him into them. They can have reason to believe that He makes appointments and keeps them.

Means of grace

To make Himself findable to us God uses, indeed we may even say He needs to use, the physical world. It is something like this that people mean when they talk, rather grandly, about "a sacramental universe". This means a universe in which matter is capable of being the bearer of spirit. Physical things are not always just "stuff" but can be laden with value. "Material" is truly "raw material" for whatever makes life significant.

The only world we know, the world we believe God made, is a world of bodies. Spirit has to be "made flesh" in some way or other to become known to us. So the idea of a "sacrament" is central: "an outward and visible sign of an inward and spiritual grace".[11] What this can mean needs to be explained quite carefully. The hope is that we may come to see the whole everyday world as able to mediate holiness to us; but it could look as if religion were doing a kind of take-over bid to make everything churchy. If we think of the sacraments that go on in church as special pious exercises, we shall not be at all enlightened to be told that the whole universe is really like this.

What happens in a sacrament is that physical "elements" are consecrated to be vehicles of holy presence. Gerard Manley Hopkins said that "the world is charged with the grandeur of God". That is one way of saying that the whole world is sacramental. In a particular sacrament, particular things are "charged" with significance.

"Sacrament" is a religious word but it becomes so because it takes up our human need to give physical expression to everything that matters to us. To hold out a hand, to make a tool, to serve a meal, to write a letter, to give a present, to make an offering, to wear a ring, to create a work of art, to receive bread and wine are all ways of endowing material things with real significance. Some but not all of them are "symbolic" acts. All of them might in a way be called sacramental. In all of them physical things are the bearers of personal presence. To "consecrate" a material object is to make it a "means of grace". The cluster of ideas of blessing, dedicating, taking and giving, have roots in the whole of human life, wherever meaning, large or small, is bestowed by personal action.

In the Christian Eucharist bread and wine are consecrated to be bearers of God's presence. Part of the meaning of the service is to be an answer to the question "Where is God?" If we believe He was truly present in Christ, then His presence is renewed here. It is a pity that the phrase "real presence" has been a battleground, when it could be so suitable for picking out the central significance of the sacrament. The Eucharist has gathered to itself all manner of meanings down the centuries, and different aspects are all-important to different people; but it ought not to be controversial to say that it is more than a mere memorial. When we celebrate the Lord's Supper we not only remember but also "re-call" his presence. The Lord ate and drank with his disciples and renewed this communion with them after his death and rising again. Not only at the Last Supper he "took bread and blessed, and broke it, and gave it to them", and by continuing to "do this"[12] they are able to be "in touch" with him still. Whatever more the Eucharist may signify, at least it is an appointment or rendezvous.

The sacrament is physically and spiritually something to take hold of. The "Eucharist" or Thanksgiving is the most "all-purpose" of its names. To give thanks over bread and wine is a way of "saying grace", blessing physical things into spiritual meaning. It is a way of keeping in touch, because here is something objectively given, not something we make up for ourselves. Whatever we feel or do not feel about it, it is there to be found, not once for all but again and again. To enter into this tradition is to do what Christians have always done. One of the earliest of all Christian pictures, in the Catacomb of St Priscilla in Rome, is the Breaking of the Bread: our fellow Christians in the second century doing what we still do. Eating and drinking together is a most profound human symbol and here it is taken into the centre of our faith. As Luther put it:

"If anyone be in despair . . . let him go joyfully to the Sacrament . . . and seek help from the entire company of the spiritual body and say, 'I have on my side Christ's Righteousness, life and sufferings with all the holy angels and all the blessed in heaven and all good men upon earth. If I die I am not alone in death. If I suffer, they suffer with me.'"[13]

We go on doing this because we believe that wherever else God is, He is findable here.

Human presence

Human beings are finite which means, partly, that they are findable in one place at a time. They are in touch with one another as individual embodied people. There is no doubt about their embodiment: it is their "spirit" which is more questionable. Are they more than bodies? Can we still say that they have "souls"? To take hold of this notion of being findable, being in touch, can be a good way to explore the complicated problems about souls and bodies.

Souls are not like Russian dolls, little figures inside us which turn out to repeat all the features of bodies. Suppose instead we try defining my soul as what it is like to be me, and my body as my presence, what I am for other people. In this way of thinking we are far from trying to abolish the soul. The "doubleness" of people is real but is not a kind of doubleness that counts against their wholeness. We can say that the twofold character of a person is like the twofold character of a window. From inside, we look out through the glass at the world, framed by the window panes. But from the outside, people look at the house and see the window itself as a thing: which it is. It is one thing with these two aspects, not two things joined. Even from inside the room, the window is still a thing we can look *at* as well as *through*.

> A man that looks on glass
> On it may stay his eye,
> Or if he pleases through it pass
> And then the heaven espy.[14]

Less metaphorically, we can say that people are living points of view. A "point of view" is an idea which starts as simply physical but can mean much more. The physical world itself can be described as a system of points of view. From every position in space, the rest of the world could be pictured from this particular perspective. You can set about imagining what it would look like from there. There are plenty of impossible perspectives for creatures such as ourselves: at the centre of the sun or in the middle of a block of wood: places where nobody, no body, can go. But plenty of perspectives are actually occupied, by animals or people. A live human body is an active centre of experiences. Somebody is in touch with the world from that perspective. When we try to imagine disembodied people, the real difficulty is to imagine people without points of view. To put myself in somebody else's *place* is to imagine what it looks like, feels like, is like, to be that person. Being myself includes touching with my own fingers, treading with my own feet, seeing with my own eyes, hearing with my own ears: or being handicapped if I am deprived of these possibilities.

When I cannot hear what you are saying I try to come nearer, or cup my hands, or use a deaf-aid to gather the sounds better into my ears. When I cannot see and the reason is that something is in the way I move it, or myself. I try to get to a "vantage point". Often my senses distort, but the distortions make a pattern. I am short-sighted or maybe I am seeing through rose-coloured spectacles. If I have a lively imagination I can see all sorts of things "in my mind's eye". I can always hope to enlarge my perspective, literally or metaphorically, but to lose my perspective would be to lose myself. When people think of somehow getting outside their bodies, they still imagine themselves with points of view. One way of asking the question of "survival" is, what happens to my point of view when it can no longer be located in my physical body?

If we say in this kind of way that my "soul" is what it is like to be me, "survival" becomes a real problem, to which the answer is not just obvious. Immortality is neither built in to the very idea of a soul nor ruled out. It makes sense to go on asking, when someone has died and his body – his presence – has gone, whether his soul can live on: in other words, whether there can be anything *for him* any more? When he died he lost his purchase on this world, but can his own particular "point of view" ever be re-embodied? Is he lost for ever or can he be found somewhere?

A gap to bridge

Thinking of souls as live viewpoints gives us a way of putting the question about survival. We need not let human hopes go by default by never quite daring to ask. Many bereaved people have pushed the idea of heaven so far into the back of their minds that they cannot, as it were, lay their hands on it. They may find it more comforting to think of someone as living on in her descendants and in the continuity of her work, and even in the memorials we put up. "In black ink my love may still shine bright."[15] Our ancestors are not wholly dead as long as we can represent them. Our benefactors are not wholly dead as long as we are grateful to them. This is good, valid comfort as far as it goes. It offers a real kind of survival apart from religious faith; but not survival of the *soul*. It is a kind of bodily presence: when someone has gone, something can remain for us; but it says nothing, either way, about what remains for the person we loved. It is not all we want. But can we have what we want?

Among all the suggested definitions of human beings as rational animals, tool-using animals, talking animals, one likely candidate might be: human beings are the animals that ask a lot from life. They are not simply contented with their terms of reference. They are apt to aspire to another existence, even to eternal life. But they do not quite know what they are asking.

Most of us want to carry on as individual people, whatever that may mean, but we have long ago put behind us any idea of simply rising from our tombs like getting up in the morning. Nor can we go back to the notion of the Almighty gathering up all the particles from here and there that made our bodies, and taking them up to the sky to float about in the clouds. That is just the sort of heaven astronauts can never find. No wonder the traditional soul has had a long run for its money as something to hook our identity on to, at least to bridge the gap between this world and the next.

The problem we need to face is that once we have given some thought to what embodiment means, the traditional soul does not seem to do this linking job. How are we to find the people we used to know when their own bodies have perished? Whatever a resurrection body is, it cannot be just like a fresh donkey for me to ride. It must be more "me" than that: but how? If it is the body that places us, that makes us findable, and the body has gone, how can we ever be *re*-placed? Or are we, as individual people, only too easily replaced: by a different lot of individuals? What right do we have to say that the new bodies really belong to the old people? Where is the continuity, once we have abandoned the idea that the new bodies will be made of the very same stuff?

For believers in ghosts, in and out of machines, these are silly questions. Continuity of consciousness, which means continuity of memory, is what makes the person. But philosophers are quick to point out that memories are just as fragile, unreliable and perishable as eyes and ears and limbs. The mind is as earthbound as the body. It does not need philosophy, only acquaintance with ageing people, to find this out. We cannot easily get away from the fact that real human life depends upon human bodies: so how can the same real person get from this world to the next?

The easiest answer for the spiritually-minded to give is that we have completely misunderstood. The next life is so different from this life that the difficulties we are worrying about simply do not apply. Heaven, they say, is not a place but a state. It is not the top floor of a three-storey universe but a condition of blessed contemplation altogether beyond the limitations of earthly life. Of course, in a way, this must be true: but it is so far beyond the present understanding of people who are not mystics as to be quite unhelpful. Its impact can be negative not positive. Spaceless, timeless beatitude comes through to the unregenerate imagination like the situation of a butterfly transfixed upon a pin. If that is eternal life, no wonder so few people really long for it. Children quickly pick up the fact that the grown-ups do not want to die. If becoming as little children has anything to do with entering the Kingdom of Heaven, it cannot be a good preparation for heaven to repudiate the naïve questions as if they were stupid as well as childish.

The naïve question "Where is heaven?" is really asking what sort of physics heaven would need for people to be in touch with one another there. What is more, it could have a respectable scientific answer. Why must a spatial system be part of *our* space? The plain idea that all space is one is like the plain idea that the earth is flat. Of course it is, the bit we live on. But the reason why we cannot come to the edge of the table and fall off is that really we live on a globe, though most of the time we can ignore this. Einstein has taught us that space itself is curved, whatever that means. At least it may open our minds to the notion that even this physical universe is not straightforward.[16] Our commonsense flat-earth geometry will do us very well, as long as we take it as provisional. When we get to the edge of experience there is no simple Q.E.D.

Suppose we say that heaven, like this world, is a system of points of view. We can picture it as a real space not joined to our space. But the question which bites hard is how a real person from here could get there. What do we think it means to say that somebody dies on earth and lives on in heaven? What departs from here and arrives there?

Philosophers can easily make us suppose that the whole idea of a "person" is problematical. They entertain one another with nightmare stories about brain transplants and split personalities, until we seem to be in a world where people's identities could be so mixed up that even God could hardly say who must be who. Suppose two people claimed to be me and one had my body and the other had my memories? Or one had my brain and the other had the rest of my body? Suppose two quite different personalities, like Dr Jekyll and Mr Hyde, seemed to be sharing my bodily frame? That after all has been known to happen. The case of "Sally Beauchamp" is apparently fact not fiction.[17] Or suppose I were somehow doubled, both physically and mentally, and each new person thought she was me? People who believe in souls can ask where, as a matter of fact, the soul has really gone. People who disbelieve in souls can look at these interesting variations with open minds. But people who believe in another life for whole persons cannot afford to be muddled about what a whole person is.

It needs saying that the puzzle cases carry more emotional weight than they deserve because they make us think of frightening developments in medicine: cloning, already possible, and brain transplants, horribly imaginable. They make us feel, rather than think, that our identity is on the brink of a precipice, even in this world. They make heaven seem impossible because once we start speculating we seem to have to let in all these unpalatable contingencies.

What we need to do is keep our heads and deal with real questions. Clones and Sally Beauchamp seem to be on the edge of our present experience: but can be dealt with more or less in terms of our present idea of a person. Clones are just identical twins writ large. Sally Beauchamp suggests that embodiment may be odder than we might expect. If she really was a distinct person we must hope that in another world she would have a body of her own: but one cannot interpret the evidence properly out of popular and semi-popular accounts. "Brain transplants" have not yet reached the sort of feasibility for us to be clear exactly what problems they would create. We must ask for more data. The surgeon has done this or that and the result was that or this: so now, how are we to interpret these given facts? But we have not yet been shown that the seemingly unanswerable questions about the replication or mixing of individual people even make sense. To ask what we ought to say if a child of God is doubled or scrambled is a little like asking how we can run a riding school when all the horses suddenly turn into elephants. We are not living in a world in which we have any reason to suppose such a possibility is coherent. This is not the argument, "Trust in God and there won't be any disasters." We might very well consider what we should do if all the horses died. Even though it seems extremely unlikely, perhaps we had better take out an insurance policy. But as for the wilder "problem cases" which are supposed to show that we do not really know what a person is, it is no wonder that they have not yet become medical problems. We do not have to jump to the conclusion that they need be a problem in the next world either.

Having refused to be stampeded, we must admit that there are plenty of difficulties. If we believe that people can live on after bodily death, we cannot escape the challenge to say what we mean by the *same* person. The temptation is to shuttle to and fro between body and soul as what really counts. When we are particularly aware that the body is mortal, we cling to the idea that the real person is the consciousness. But then we realize that the continuity of our consciousness is as fragile as the continuity of our bodies, that memory can be deceptive and that people need bodies for other people to find and identify them. Then we produce resurrection as a kind of trump card. Our religion has always taught that we shall have the bodies we need. But then we are asked whether the resurrection body will have to be just like the person we knew, and we remember that the last time we saw Mr Smith he was frail and incapacitated, both mentally and physically. Then we swing back to the "soul" again, though we seem to be able to say nothing about it except that it is sacred and immortal. With bodies so perishable and consciousness so vulnerable, it begins to seem no wonder that so many people decide that "the noes have it".

FOR REFLECTION

Rudolf Otto, *The Idea of the Holy*, OUP 1950, Appendix VIII

. . . Scripture knows no "Omnipresence", neither the expression nor the meaning it expresses; it knows only the God who is where He wills to be, and is not where He wills not to be . . . an august mystery, that comes and goes, approaches and withdraws, has its time and hour, and may be far or near in infinite degrees, "closer than breathing" to us or miles remote from us . . .

St Augustine, *Confessions*, Book VII:10

. . . And Thou didst beat back the weakness of my sight, shining forth upon me thy dazzling beams of light, and I trembled with love and fear. I realized that I was far away from Thee in the land of unlikeness, as if I heard Thy voice from on high: "I am the food of strong men; grow and you shall feed on Me; nor shall you change Me, like the food of your flesh into yourself, but you shall be changed into My likeness . . ."

Austin Farrer, "The Eucharist in 1 Corinthians", *Eucharistic Theology then and now*, SPCK Theological Collections 1968, p. 31

He gave them the sacrament by eating with them; he made it their salvation by his death.

Queen Elizabeth I

> His was the word that spake it,
> He took the bread and brake it,
> And what his word did make it
> I do believe and take it.

Austin Farrer, *Saving Belief*, Hodder and Stoughton 1964, p. 145

Space is a web of interactions between material energies which form a system by thus interacting.

. . . heaven can be as dimensional as it likes, without ever getting pulled into our spatial field, or having any possible contact with us of any physical kind. . . . How I wish we could explain the Einsteinian theory to St Augustine!

7

Patterns of Lovability

Finding and minding

It is worth noticing that commonsense is not too worried about what "person" means. We simply think we know what our personal identity is, even if we cannot give any account of it which will stand up to philosophical analysis. We may find it hard to believe in resurrection, but not because we fear we would not know who we were or which was our new body. We can imagine ourselves waking up again after death embodied or disembodied, and coming to terms with this new existence whatever it turns out to be like: heavenly, hellish or purgatorial, or maybe reincarnated in another mortal life. We should be upset if we wake up in Valhalla. Most of us are ill-adapted to enjoy the happy hunting grounds. Some of us have all the wrong skills for the conventional Christian heaven. But we are not talking about square circles.

The reason why commonsense is not too worried is that commonsense is not afraid of making howlers, until tutored into shuddering at them. Critical thought proceeds by discovering howlers, disowning them, and then, sometimes, rehabilitating them. Christian thinkers are prone to take it to be their duty to make strenuous efforts to rehabilitate ghostly souls living in machines, but perhaps they are making the wrong howler.

To understand what a person really is, we do not need ghosts in machines. What we do need is to be allowed to link up values and facts. It has been a standard lesson for philosophy students that they must never, never try to get an "ought" from an "is". It has been a useful lesson up to a point. Some muddles have been avoided and some arguments shown up as unsound. One has learnt not to make risky jumps from given facts to moral precepts, such as "They say so. So we must obey". But this lesson has been overdone. The world is not as tidy as it suggests. Facts are hardly ever really "value-free". When we try to keep facts and values so rigidly apart, whole areas of human life are ruled out of bounds. Even when we are talking about what most matters to us, we have learnt to leave out the very fact that it matters. When we are talking about souls, immortal or otherwise, we are careful not to mention that we love them, let alone to suggest that God loves them.

Surely this makes a difference to the question, "How do we identify the same person, in this world or the next?" Last time we saw Mr Smith he was frail and incapacitated: so if we meet a bonny bouncing Mr Smith tomorrow we hardly suppose it is the same person. It must be Mr Smith Junior. But in heaven everyone must be bonny and bouncing, so how can we recognize anybody? The fact that we call him Mr Smith, or in a good many arguments of this sort, Mr X,[1] gives away the whole case. Who cares whether a theoretical Mr Smith or Mr X goes on living or not? Does it matter what we decide about whether he must have the same body or the same brain or make the right memory claims? The people we mind about, whose destiny is important to us, do not have to be recognized by set criteria. We do not give so many points for face and so many for voice; nor even so many for authentic reminiscence. We read off a pattern from all the signs that are given to us. People can reveal their presence in many ways, by touch, by telephone and perhaps even by telepathy. "I should know her anywhere", we say. Of course we make mistakes. Mary Magdalene takes the Lord for the gardener, until he calls her by her name.[2] Tom Smith's real identity, we may say, is his love: his concern: his minding, not just his mind. What is actual and recognizable in us is more than material particles, more than a stream of consciousness. It is the pattern of our value to ourselves and to other people. The fact of the person is not complete, even as a fact, without the value of the person. St Augustine said, "My weight is my love".[3] The living human being is lovable human being. "Love" is a word we are nervous or embarrassed to use nowadays in serious discussions, because it has been so much sentimentalized and cheapened: but we need it here. It is accurate not sentimental to describe a person as a living pattern of love.[4]

The person I am is not just the cells I am made of at present. In seven years' time, they say, I shall have an entirely new set. The person I am is not just my fragile memories. I am not just my mind. The person I am is the person whose mattering I know at first hand, the person I mind about, whether I like it or not, with a particular kind of regard which is basic and maybe indefinable. The people we recognize are fellow matterers. They matter to themselves; they matter to us; and above all, Christians believe, they matter to God.

What we need to risk saying about people is that they are meeting points of fact and value. Whatever really matters in the universe matters to people. In particular, people themselves matter. This is where the "howler" comes in: we must dare to say at this point that somehow or other the *value* of people is a *fact*. It is the main fact about them, and if we cannot see this we have not really understood what people are.

This way of approach to the idea of the soul makes sense of our "doubleness". We are indeed bodies and souls. Bodies in their nature are findable, and now we are saying that souls in their nature are, so to say, "mindable". The soul is not something left over when the body has gone. It is not a sort of remainder "carried forward" when one's mortal frame has perished. It is the whole person considered as the seat of value.

Some of the words we use about people have a sort of ambiguity which allows them to move backwards and forwards between body and soul, fact and value. We say people are sensitive, and sensitivity can be a plain reaction to a stimulus, jerking away from a pinpoint, or a graceful response to a fellow human being. We give importance to relationship, which may be of many kinds from the geometrical to the romantic. Bonds can be of gratitude as well as of rope. It is almost impossible to use the word "heart" to mean a mere pump. These may be metaphors but they are not puns. They are bridge words between facts and values. It is not surprising that we keep on needing to talk in these ways.

One of these bridge notions is an idea which has played a part in this argument already, the idea of a "point of view". A point of view is a point in space, a findable place. Where something is to be found is a "value-free fact", if we like. But if it is a point *of view* it is an occupied place. There is somebody there, somebody who might get in touch with us. "In touch" is another of these linking words. It moves from the geometrical idea of a tangent, by way of the material idea of a contact, towards the human idea of a communication. So the concept of a person edges its way in, and the physical slides into the moral. Once we recognize people we begin to say, with hardly a jump, that their points of view matter. Facts are not value-free any more. But we have not arrived in a different world. We are still in the same physical world which we regard from our different perspectives, now somehow deepened or thickened up to make room for what really matters to us.

This way of letting value into fact is not just a trick. The idea of a conscious viewpoint simply will not stay neutral. Surely it is impossible to imagine a consciousness that did not matter at all, or a conscious being that did not mind in the least what it was conscious of? A creature does not have to have a full-scale *mind* to be capable of *minding*. The smallest consciousness can begin to have something we could call "wants". From "wants" it is a short step to "purposes", and from "purposes" to "values".

There is literally a world of difference between a speck of dust at a particular place and an ant occupying that place. If you tread on an ant, that is the end of the ant's world. We may well say this does not matter, because the ant does not mind dying. It does not "look before and after". We hope that an ant's consciousness is so marginal that eliminating it does not matter; but it would matter to pull off its legs. Most people would jib at saying that an ant had rights or a soul, but if it has a point of view it can have, so to speak, wrongs. If a creature can be hurt, something more than physical science comes in. Of course this is much more evidently true when one considers the point of view of a dog or an ape. Many of us believe that some animals are, as it were, honorary members of our moral world. Somewhere along the line from an amoeba to a human being we begin to need the concept of the soul: not as a kind of physical thing separable from the body, but as the easiest way to reckon with the spiritual aspect of a creature of God.

Continuing the progress from neutral facts to full-scale values, we may take a further step. We can scarcely imagine a collection of conscious beings, conscious of themselves and of one another, who would not begin to understand that other people had wants too.

They begin to become able to enter into somebody else's point of view. They begin, we may say, to mind about each other. So we can dare to suggest that the fact of consciousness can let love into the world. That is what it really means to say that people are meeting points of fact and value. With open eyes we do need to get "ought" from "is".

Soul-making

We need the idea of the soul. It is the simplest way of talking about the spiritual aspect of a human being. A person is a soul. Each of us is a moving pattern of minding and mattering, capable of relationships with other people. Indeed Christians will say that relationships with God and people are what we are made for. It is better not to say that a person *has* a soul, as if the soul were a separate part of us that could flourish, or manage, on its own.

If we think on these lines the idea of the world as a "vale of soul-making" is most congenial. John Keats, so distrustful of orthodox Christianity that he thought he was being heretical, arrived at it in a letter to his brother George in America. There may, he said, be "sparks of the divinity in millions", and he asked, "How then are souls to be made? How then are these sparks which are God to have identity given them – so as ever to possess a bliss peculiar to each one's individual existence? How, but by the medium of a world like this?"[5]

Keats offered this suggestion as a way of making sense of our condition and our aspirations, not, of course, as a scientific hypothesis. Christians have every right to find it attractive. The notion of our real kinship to God does not have to be suspect; though maybe Eastern Orthodox believers, who have thought about our goal as "deification",[6] might be more able to

The Hope Of Heaven

give it a fair hearing than Westerners, who have often shied away from any such idea.

As for the notion of the soul as something developing rather than all-or-nothing, we now need this more flexible idea even more than Keats did. If we had to say that "the soul" was a gift of God all complete, probably given at the moment of conception, then the slow evolution of human beings from the animal creation would really be as awkward a challenge as Darwin's contemporaries feared. For if our religious belief demands that a creature either definitely has or definitely has not a soul, then we are required to go in for a mind-boggling racism about the borderline cases. Did Neanderthal man have a soul? If we count him in, as homo sapiens, then do we count homo erectus out? Wherever we draw the line, we find ourselves somewhere with a child who is counted in and a parent who has to be counted out. But if we allow for "soul-making" then there can be souls half-made and "patterns of lovability" being formed. The question is not, "Does this one qualify?" but "Can we glimpse God's love for this creature?"

Nothing prevents us from saying that the human soul is sacred,[7] provided we do not try to treat "sacredness" as a kind of celestial birth certificate, which somehow both guarantees indestructibility and also makes destruction into sacrilege. It may sound odd to suggest that "sacredness" might be a matter of degree, and plenty of problems arise; but they are real problems, "What are we to do about this fellow creature?" rather than legalistic questions, "Is this creature 'one of us', or not?"

This flexibility matters, because the "borderline cases" are not just a handful of individuals who can be treated as exceptions. The evolution of human beings took millions of years. There were generations and generations of what used to be called "missing links", who are not entirely missing any more, whose bones are being found and whose ways of life are being deduced. We cannot any longer do with notions of the soul which would seem to tie God's hands about the destiny of all these creatures who lived and struggled and cherished their offspring, experienced pleasures and pains, and died after a short life-span. We must, of course, be able to say that God knows what fulfilment He has in store for all of them. We can put them alongside those fully human beings who never arrive at human living because they are too handicapped, or perish too soon. God has all eternity to bring any of His creatures, along with us, to satisfying maturity. We can understand this better if we think of developing "patterns of lovability" rather than the presence or absence of "immortal souls".

Resurrection

We may face the fact that there is no such thing as an "immortal soul", an unkillable spirit made to live for ever, whatever happens. A "matterer" could die. A "pattern of lovability" could come to an end. Plenty of people who are not in the least "materialist" in their values believe sadly that this is the human condition, that we shall all come to an end, that our souls die with our bodies. Christians are apt to suppose that the answer is a sturdy reaffirmation of immortal souls. But surely Christians ought to put their hopes, not in "souls" but in God. Instead of pinning our faith to immortality as a possession of ours, we trust, much more coherently, in the power and mercy of God. The Creator who made us can remake us without needing to salvage our broken fragments.

Some people have such a lively belief in the next world that for them the problem has not arisen. They are able to picture the people they love who have died

The Hope Of Heaven

simply transferred to heaven, like a kind of exciting emigration. They go on thinking of them and praying for them as if they had gone to live in the tropics. No letters are going to come, but one day we shall all follow and our dear ones will be there to meet us and show us round. But for many of us, the imminent prospect of death for a real person who is part of our life shakes this easy hope. Especially if the approach to death includes clouding of mind as well as weakening of body, our imaginations and our intellects tell us that dying really is more comprehensive than falling asleep on a night journey all ready to wake up somewhere else. "He has gone" feels true, and the euphemisms like "called to higher service" do not comfort.

To find our real hope we need to relinquish the dubious hope. We can afford to accept that there may be a time when the person we loved is nowhere. We need not try to persuade ourselves that our own "souls" can never be extinguished. What we believe is that the God who made the people who matter to us is able at His pleasure to remake whatever physical or mental frames are needed to express those particular "patterns of lovability". He can put us in touch so that we can go on minding about one another. According to this way of thinking, what I may hope to be in the next world is not an indestructible consciousness somehow attached to some kind of replica of my present body cured of its disabilities, but the distinctive pattern of spiritual, physical and mental life I know and am known by.

What I recognize when I recognize the same person, in this world or another, is a pattern of personality I have interacted with and maybe helped to form. Sometimes recognition is immediate, sometimes it takes a little while. The bodily shape helps but is not essential. When the telephone rings I hear a friend's familiar voice, but more particularly I find myself in a conversation I understand. The other person is there. If

I cough, I almost expect to give her my germs; although I know that her presence is being mediated by electrical impulses and maybe she is hundreds of miles away. Surely God can be a better physicist than Telecom when it comes to putting His children in touch with one another?

A good analogy is available now to explain what resurrection might mean. We may say that body and soul are like the hardware and the software of a computer.[8] The soul is not a ghost sitting in a machine but a program capable of being reactivated, even maybe after a long pause. The point of the analogy is that we can have the very same program without it being necessary to have the very same stuff, whether "hardware" or "software". The program can be stored in various ways, may be copied, and fed into a different computer after a gap. During the gap the program is completely out of action. So we can get rid of the idea that when my body dies "I" must somehow be still alive if I am to survive. What I need is for someone to preserve the pattern of my existence and eventually to reactivate me in a compatible body.

But suppose the same program were fed into two separate computers? Would there be two of me? This difficulty has been called the "Replica Objection"[9] and has been much canvassed by philosophers as a possibly fatal argument against resurrection. It is a matter of what right we can have to say that a person really is the *same person* across a gap. The body is quite similar, the memories are quite convincing: but can we be *sure*? The answer so far has been: if it is someone you love you can be sure, as sure as you are now, and for the same reasons. The "value-free" person is a needless myth leading to needless nightmares. But the philosophical niggle remains. Suppose there were two, which would it be? By what right do I say that there *could* not be two?

A Christian will robustly answer, "Indeed there could not be two replicas of one person, because only God can remake the one person and we can trust Him not to do it twice." Before this answer can satisfy, it will be necessary to say a good deal more about what we mean by this trusting and by this remaking.

Here the argument forks, like a path in a wood. We hope to explore both ways, but can only take one at a time. Before coming back to the discussion of remaking,[10] that is of what "resurrection" can mean without "immortal souls", it is necessary to produce some justification for saying any of this at all. What right can we have to talk about trusting God to raise us up again?

People who believe in immortal souls may not see the problem in this form. For them, the human soul is the kind of thing that naturally goes on existing, and belief in God can be vaguer and less dogmatic. But if on the contrary there is no part of us which is immortal, then everything depends on God. Whatever hope we have must be definitely theological. The time has come to "talk shop".

FOR REFLECTION

David Jenkins, *The Glory of Man*, SCM 1967, pp. 2–3
I assume one ground which I take to be self-evident, universal and inescapable. I assume that our concern is with persons. If it is not, then I assert that our concern *ought* to be with persons. To refuse or ignore this concern is a failure to face up to what is involved in being a human being . . . You must consider in what ways it matters to you to be you, keeping your investigation in the first person.

John Austin Baker, *The Foolishness of God*, DLT 1970, p. 287
If God is to give us a life after death, therefore, we must assume that this pattern is preserved by Him to serve as the formative principle of the re-created being. In that sense the "soul" never dies.

G.R. Dunstan, "A Theologian's Reflections on some Areas of Surgical Practice" in *Matters of Life and Death*, ed. Shotter, DLT 1970, p. 59
"The soul", we might say, is human personality conceived of relationally.

8

The Resurrection

By what right?

In emphasizing resurrection rather than immortality, at least we can claim not to be flying in the face of our tradition: far from it. Reading the Bible – Old Testament and New – tends to confirm the belief that the body is just as necessary to the human being as any separable "soul". At one time more would have been made of this point, and the "Hebrew" cast of mind praised more than the "Greek". There is a reaction now against this over-simplified contrast, but it is still true that the conviction that body and spirit belong together finds more encouragement in the Scriptures than in Plato.

When Christ was asked about the resurrection, we are told, he did not reply, "Of course there is a resurrection: you have immortal souls"; but nor did he avoid giving a straight answer. He talked, as we should put it, about relationship, about God saying to Moses, "I am the God of Abraham, Isaac and Jacob"; and the climax of the story is that "He is not the God of the dead, but the God of the living".[1] It is in keeping with this tradition and with much else in the gospels to say, not that people are immortal, but that God will raise them up. It is because they matter to Him that He will not let them perish.

Of course this is hard to believe, and when we are asked what right we have to believe it we point to the resurrection of Christ. We believe God can raise the dead because He did. Christ's rising is the pledge that ours is possible. But if we assert this so baldly we are moving much too fast. The path of the argument forks here again. There are problems, both about what Christ's rising means, and about how it relates to ours.

What Christ's rising means might be thought obvious, and to make it a bone of contention merely faithless. People who take sophisticated views about what happened at the first Easter are abused, when they give public voice to them, as "not believing in the Resurrection". Part of the trouble, but not all, has been a failure of communication. Radicals have been mistaken for sceptics; and indeed, when radicals behave like Cordelia and refuse to make positive affirmations, it is little wonder that their statements are taken for denials.

It would be easy to moralize about the condition of a church in which such misunderstandings arise, but moralizing would be particularly unhelpful because it is partly a kind of "moralism" which has brought us where we are. Christians have been ill-equipped to cope with questions about the foundation of our belief because of a sort of pervasive assumption that the Christian faith is *all* about being good. The message is sometimes the values of our ancestors and the upholding of standards, rather than the Cross and Resurrection of the Lord. To be fair, the characteristic Christian moral emphasis is put upon self-sacrificing love, so that the Cross does become the centre of everything: but it still is not made clear why the Cross is *good* news.

The Resurrection has somehow tended to get lost in the lumber-room of people's minds, not thrown away but dusty and crumpled. They cannot lay their hands on it in a hurry, but they react with fury if anyone seems to suggest that it has gone for good. Or maybe it is like one of those very holy pictures in Italian churches which has a permanent little curtain over it and is not shown to the public. Is it still there or has it been put in a museum?

The idea that God positively did something, that the Gospel is not just a set of ideals but a real matter of fact, is quite frightening to twentieth-century people who cannot go back to being scientific and philosophical innocents. There is a strong temptation not to affirm or deny the Resurrection, but to cover it up for safety. So it disappears from view until somebody asks what has happened to it, and panic ensues. But unless the affirmation that "The Lord is risen" means something definite, we cannot go on to make it the basis of our hope. Having appealed to resurrection rather than immortality, we are obliged to enter the current discussion about what *the* Resurrection was.

Preconceptions and concerns

There is not just a simple choice here between scepticism and faith. Among people who do want to make the Christian affirmation that the Lord is risen we can distinguish at least three ways of trying to interpret this announcement: subjective, spiritual and literal.

There are theologians today who believe in God and want to call themselves Christians but who cannot cope with the notion of "the supernatural". They find it impossible to believe that something miraculous happened to Jesus when he was dead. For these people it is miracle enough that something happened to the followers of Jesus. For them the Easter Gospel is that the disciples got their courage back and saw that what the Lord stood for is more important than death. The Lord lives in our hearts when we love one another, and that, they say, is what Resurrection means: as real to us as it was to the first generation of Christians.

This account is not offered as a caricature, though it is hard to be fair to a view one finds incredible. It seems that for some it is strong enough to be a faith to live and die by. It must be said though that if it were the truth, the Resurrection would be precisely a non-event. An enormous weight has to be put on Christian consciousness of being restored and renewed, because on this view our rising has to be the pledge of Christ's, and not vice versa. We have lost the one mighty act of God which was to be the basis for our hopes.

If people do want to go on being Christians although they believe that the Resurrection of Christ was a non-event, heaven forbid that more traditional Christians should unchurch them and try to deprive them of the faith they have; but nor may these would-be believers usurp the authority of "assured conclusions" for their subjective re-interpretation of the Gospel. It is still a diminished understanding of the Christian faith, a *faute de mieux*, to maintain that Jesus lives only in the hearts of his followers and reigns only from the Cross.

Surely the first disciples believed and proclaimed that something had happened to Jesus, not only to themselves. Does the Easter faith therefore mean that what happened was the Empty Tomb? This is where disciples today are beset by failures of communication.

For a moment the course of this argument looks obvious. We have been insisting upon the importance of the whole person, body and "soul" together, not in separation. It must be granted that the whole person is as mortal as we know the body is; and therefore any hope we have for a life after death must lie in the power and love of God. But now we have to check the argument from running away with us. Here at the centre of our faith is this proclamation that the power and love of God did the very thing we ask and raised up His Son, body and soul together, as a pledge that He can and will raise all His children. What more can we ask? But then we have learned Christian theologians coming along and teaching that the Empty Tomb is incredible. Are they not cutting off the branch we are all sitting on? Must we not resist them with every argument we can muster?

That would be too quick a jump to a congenial conclusion. The failures of communication need more exploration first. It must be stated, even if it sounds both obvious and patronizing, that the "spiritual" and the "literal" believers in the Resurrection of Christ each have a positive case which needs to be heard. Neither side is to be dismissed, either as superstitious or as unbelieving. A dogged determination to take our sources at face value is not the only kind of Christian integrity.

Sometimes it is assumed that there is only one way of affirming the Resurrection: that unless the Lord simply got up and walked out of the tomb the whole story would be a "myth" in the everyday sense of myth which means fiction. People who look for a more complicated belief in a real resurrection of a more "spiritual" kind, based mainly on the appearances of Christ, have not succeeded in explaining themselves to their fellow Christians. Their denials have been heard; their affirmations have been too unobtrusive to be heeded. So they have been lumped in with the people who try to explain the Resurrection away.

What they are really doing is putting their faith in the Risen Christ who made himself known.[2] They emphasize that the Empty Tomb is a late strand in the stories. So, they say, it is the appearances of the Lord, with all their vitality and strangeness, which are fundamental. They point out that St Paul does not seem to know anything about the Empty Tomb: but there is nothing "merely subjective" about his preaching of the Resurrection. His is the earliest witness we have, with a ringing definiteness that Christ died, was buried, was raised on the third day, appeared to his followers and last of all to Paul himself "as to one untimely born".[3]

The arguments about the meaning of this testimony go on, just because it is so weighty. Did Paul, or did he not, count the appearance to himself as an appearance like the others in his list, or a special visitation? Does the phrase "on the third day" refer to the Empty Tomb after all, or does it not? One cannot help thinking that the answers people give to these questions are bound to depend to some extent on their existing convictions about the possibility and likelihood of God's working by a physical miracle. There is nothing disreputable about this. Of course our presuppositions weigh with us, when the evidence is so delicately poised, and of course there is nothing disreputable about people who believe in God having a presupposition in favour of miracles. So we can no more write off the traditionalists as naïve than we can write off the radicals as heretical. We may well say "God knows". Our notions are approximations.

If we have a presupposition in favour of the wholeness of the person, we shall naturally feel that the Empty Tomb is a help not a hindrance. To affirm it still looks like the most straightforward and complete way of being a Christian. The traditional creed has a robustness worthy of its purpose. Among all the detailed critical arguments which daunt all but biblical experts, the theological argument stands out, that belief in a physical resurrection is in keeping with the doctrine of creation. It is the raising of the *body* of the Lord that most evidently vindicates the wholeness of human life and the goodness of the physical world. Whatever we say about the Resurrection, at any rate we must not suggest that the Risen Lord was a ghost who left his machine behind. This is not an "It ought to be so, therefore it is so" argument. It is part of a whole interpretation of the way things are which claims to be coherent.

Why then are some Christians, believers in God and followers of Christ, so reluctant to affirm that on the first Easter morning the tomb was found empty? There is more at stake here than a habit, whether scholarly or faint-hearted, of disbelieving in miracles. The preconceptions that make some Christian theologians so willing to interpret the evidence differently are not all negative.

It is time to try to explain that the questions about the role of the physical body cut both ways, and it may not be only traditionalists who care about these questions. The problems about what Christ's rising means and about how it relates to ours come together again here.[4]

Christ the first fruits

The trouble with a "spiritual" view of the Resurrection is that it does not plainly vindicate our physical existence. But the "literal" view has difficulty here too. If the Lord's body did indeed get up and leave the tomb we still need to ask what encouragement his resurrection gives to us who are surely going to "see corruption".[5] How does the Gospel redeem us from Claudio's fear that to die means, for us, "to lie in cold obstruction and to rot"? A straightforward statement that the tomb was empty easily gives the impression that the Lord was brought back from the dead by being miraculously resuscitated; and resuscitation does not have much to do with eternal life. If the Lord conquered death simply by, as it were, getting up betimes, then it is hard to see how he conquered death for us all. We know for certain that we cannot expect our dead bodies to be reanimated. But if on the other hand his body stayed in the tomb, and it was just what is usually called his "soul" that appeared to the disciples, then the physical world is not vindicated and matter does not

94

matter. So there are problems both ways. There is more work to be done to integrate the historical foundation of our belief with the affirmations we go on to make.

"Christ is risen from the dead: and become the first fruits of them that slept".[6] We have put St Paul's statement into our Easter Anthems. Said or sung, it has been found a thoroughly satisfactory way of proclaiming our faith. But if what rising from the dead means is simply the reanimation of a dead body, why is the widow's son at Nain, or Lazarus, or for that matter the little boy restored to life by Elisha, not thought of as "first fruits" of the power of God to raise the dead?[7] The questions one asked as a child are not always too silly to be asked again when one has grown up. Of course we must understand that the rising of the Lord is quite different from a marvellous healing. He rose to a new kind of life. But this simply emphasizes the question, was the reanimation of his earthly body necessary for this, or an extra? Asking these questions is not impertinent. There is nothing reverent about acquiescing in a muddle. The clearest thinking we are capable of may lead us up to a mystery, but confusion sticks us where we are.

Whether our tendency is to believe as much as we can of what the first Christians handed down to us, or to see how much of it we can dispense with while still counting ourselves believers, we must reckon with the strangeness of the whole impression the Resurrection accounts give. Not surprisingly, the Lord is not to be tabulated. On the one hand there is the emphasis on the risen body. Even if we leave out the empty tomb, we are not encouraged to think of the Risen Christ as any kind of hallucination. "Handle me and see" is one definite theme.[8] But there is no simplicity here. Meeting the Risen Lord is not just like meeting Jesus of Nazareth as he was. He comes and goes mysteriously, sometimes through closed doors. He is not always recognized immediately. Mary Magdalene supposes him to be the gardener.[9] On the way to Emmaus "their eyes were kept from recognizing him".[10] The oddness of this cuts both ways. It hardly suggests a vision any more than a down-to-earth encounter. When people see visions they are generally quite clear who is appearing to them.

Another childish puzzle can bring the problem to a head. If the bodily continuity is to be of great significance to us, how do we suppose that the Risen Lord was dressed? Was he a physical man in visionary clothes? We must say, of course, that his body was transformed, but did the transformation include the arrival of suitable apparel? The questions are not frivolous, as we can see if we take them a stage further. Do we really think that this physical body went literally *up* to heaven at the Ascension, or if not what became of it? Did it arrive somewhere else in the universe, or was it after all miraculously annihilated?

It begins to look inadequate either to affirm or deny that the Risen Lord had the very same body which lay in the tomb. Resuscitation is not what we need, and yet if we give up the body we seem to be left with a ghost which is not what we need either. A coherent affirmation of the Resurrection will have to come to terms with why we both do and do not want to think of it as the reanimation of a corpse.

Letting go

Besides saying that Christ was "the first fruits of them that slept", St Paul asserted firmly that "flesh and blood cannot inherit the kingdom of God".[11] We still find this an unpalatable lesson. We have to learn it, but we are also right to find it unpalatable, because it seems to go against our certainty that the body does matter.

The Resurrection

It is only too understandable that some human beings have made desperate attempts to keep their bodies in order after death, ready for another life. Reports of cancer patients across the Atlantic arranging to be frozen in hopes of a cure are hardly different in principle from ancient Egyptians arranging to be mummified as their one chance of living on. Neither, perhaps, has been morbidly preoccupied with death, so much as hopelessly in love with life. It sounds complacent maybe, but is necessary, to say where these attempts at the perpetuation of life go wrong. The mistake, surely, is to think of death as something that could be staved off, if only we could perfect our processes of conservation.

Oddly enough, some very different people, those ascetics who have tried to win eternal life by ill-treating their bodies, have made a sort of mirror image of the same mistake. They understood very well that the body is perishable, and concluded that the proper way to proceed was to concentrate on keeping the soul. With hindsight we can see that they too were trying to cherish a part of the person rather than the whole. Simply to call them morbid would be superficial.

What we need to say, and can say in the light of the Christian faith, is that neither body nor soul can be preserved by such desperate measures, that both must die if they are to rise from the dead. The best way to understand death and resurrection is still the analogy of the grain and the wheat, propounded by St Paul and spelt out in the Fourth Gospel in the discourse of Jesus when the Greeks came to see him. "What you sow does not come to life unless it dies." "Unless a grain of wheat falls into the earth and dies, it remains alone; but if it dies, it bears much fruit."[12] In other words, the good news of the Resurrection is not about the conservation of the body at all. Mummification is precisely not the point, however technically efficient. For all the trouble expended upon it, it clearly never was technically efficient. Nobody could want to live for ever with the body of a mummy. But in any case it could not be the foundation of eternal life. Whatever the Resurrection of the Lord was, it was something entirely different from the perfect case of preservation of human remains, doing miraculously what mummification fails to do scientifically.

The point of the Resurrection is that the Lord's body does not remain. The message is: *He is not here*. He has gone. His followers cannot embalm him, cherish his relics, lay their own bodies near his, raise a monument over his bones, bring flowers, provide him with grave goods, or do any of the reverent, sad or celebratory acts that human beings do for the bodies of their dead. His body is simply not available. It is not to be made into the kind of focus of respect or love, the kind of second-best presence, that survivors hanker for. The Gospel of the Resurrection is that substitutes of this sort are neither necessary nor possible. Whatever we believe happened on the first Easter morning, the tomb of the Lord has been empty ever since in the sense that he has gone from it. We cannot find him there.[13]

People who visit the Church of the Holy Sepulchre in Jerusalem often come back disappointed and distressed. Human beings have made something deplorable of it, and the atmosphere seems all wrong for the holiest place of our religion. We do well to be deeply saddened by the ill-will and the strife: but not, surely, by the palpable absence of the Lord. The absence is the point. He is not there. He is risen.

In contrast to the Holy Sepulchre there is a tomb in the Kremlin. They have mummified Lenin and put him under a slab in Red Square, and made his tomb secure by setting a guard. It is human and reverent to honour holy relics and holy places, and not to be decried. But when one sees the contrast between the heavy granite tomb of Lenin and the exuberant domes of the Church of St Basil across the square, it seems fair to reflect that our Lord could not be kept under a slab. Christians can afford to relinquish the earthly body because they believe God can raise up the beloved human being.

So belief in the Empty Tomb can become less of a problem. Christians who found their faith upon it and Christians who find it incredible are not, after all, so far apart in their essential affirmations. First let us go along with the mainstream of our tradition and assert that the Empty Tomb is indeed the basis of the Easter faith. Then we believe that the absence of the body of the Lord was miraculous. But the miracle did not have to be a resuscitation. It was not an especially remarkable healing of a body which had gone too far in affliction and slipped over into what we call death, from which it just might be brought back. Resurrection does not come back but goes on. It is based, if one believes in this manner in the Empty Tomb, on a total departure, a completion of the process of mortality. We can say that the Lord did not "see corruption": his body did not linger in the interim condition most mortal bodies undergo. We can also say, as readily, that he is the "first fruits". He went through death as completely as we must. His rising is able to be the pledge of ours, for it is founded, as ours will have to be, upon a thoroughgoing absence.

Let me say that I find myself able to believe the traditionalist view that there was a miracle, if it can be understood in this sort of way. Of course this depends on a preconception that God could do miracles, and that this case, if any at all, is special enough to allow belief that He would. But many people, including many biblical scholars, do none the less find themselves obliged to be more radical. As they see it, the conviction that "The Lord is risen" came first, so that the stories of the tomb being empty were just one way of trying to spell it out. Such a view is much more widely held today than some traditional Christians realize.[14] Of course it is imperative that radical Christians should not dodge the question of what, if not the Empty Tomb itself, is the foundation of their resurrection faith. But provided that they can indeed answer this, their difference from the traditionalists is less than we might fear. There is an agnosticism about what happened to the Lord's body, but it has still gone. The Risen Lord is not a reanimated corpse but a re-embodied person. His presence to the first Christians had nothing to do with the rather desperate comfort of hanging on to something which has departed, but the confidence that he himself was with them again.

Whether or not we are inclined to interpret our sources literally, we do not have to be in trouble over the Ascension. We need a *doctrine* of the Ascension. It is important to affirm that when the Lord had triumphantly revealed his victory over death he ceased to be locally present to a few of his followers, so that he could become supernaturally available to all. Plenty of sermons can be preached on this theme. "Touch me not" are the words of the Risen Christ to Mary Magdalene.[15] He was recognized in the breaking of the bread at Emmaus and then "vanished out of their sight".[16] The Ascension story itself[17] need not be as naïve as people suppose. It does not require a "three-storey universe". The departure into a cloud could be a solemn goodbye, with only a restrained element of miracle. What seems impossible to believe is that the Lord took with him into the sky the body which had lain in the tomb. But if that body had gone, as mortal bodies go, his *risen* body need not be confined by our physics. Whether the tomb was miraculously empty or not, the bits of matter which made up the mortal body of Jesus may be still dispersed somewhere on this earth, and we need not be upset at the thought. The cells which become a human being change continuously; and it cannot be an irreverent thought that the Lord had growing hair and fingernails. It is part of the idea of Incarnation that matter can be consecrated for spiritual purposes.

In giving reasons for the hope that is in them traditionalists and radicals alike do well to put a lot of weight on St Paul's witness that the Lord died, was raised and appeared; and also on his analogy of the seed and the plant. Analogies cannot prove; but to explain what something can mean may go a long way towards making it convincing. The seed and plant analogy helps to explain that the emphasis of the Christian Gospel is not on conservation either of a body or a soul, but on letting go in readiness for new life. What is sown is "bare grain";[18] what is raised is something new; and we may well consider that this applies to the Lord's death as well as to ours. Surely the appearances were of what St Paul called a "spiritual body":[19] neither ghost nor vision on the one hand, nor plain flesh and blood on the other.

FOR REFLECTION

John Austin Baker, *The Foolishness of God*, DLT 1970, p. 267

The purport of the resurrection events was not just to vindicate in a general way a man and his life and teaching; it was to specify the crucified human body as the means by which that vindication was fully and finally won.

St Paul, 1 Corinthians 15:1–8 (R.S.V.)

Now I would remind you, brethren, in what terms I preached to you the Gospel, which you received, in which you stand, by which you are saved, if you hold it fast – unless you believed in vain.

For I delivered to you as of first importance what I also received, that Christ died for our sins in accordance with the scriptures, that he was buried, that he was raised on the third day in accordance with the scriptures, and that he appeared to Cephas, then to the twelve. Then he appeared to more than five hundred brethren at one time, most of whom are still alive, though some have fallen asleep. Then he appeared to James, then to all the apostles. Last of all, as to one untimely born, he appeared also to me.

George Herbert

> I got me flowers to straw thy way;
> I got me boughs off many a tree:
> But thou wast up by break of day,
> And brought'st thy sweets along with thee.

Presence Again

Taking absence seriously

What can spiritual bodies be for us? What has the rising of the Lord to do with our own rising? We have surely abandoned the notion that our resurrection, whatever it is, requires the reconstitution of the bodies we have now. So does it help to suggest that the resurrection of Christ did not have to depend upon the straightforward persistence of his body?

What we put our faith in if we believe that the Lord truly rose from the dead is a presence superimposed upon an absence. The theme is not a new one. We could say that the Resurrection is the third time it has conspicuously occurred in our tradition.

First, long before the coming of Christ, the people of God were taught not to suppose that they could capture the presence of the Almighty in images made with hands. They were not allowed to focus their worship upon a cult statue. The Ark of the Covenant, their most holy object, contained the tablets of the Law, not an idol. After the exile, when the Ark had gone, the Holy of Holies, the most sacred inner chamber of the Temple, was solemnly kept empty. Its emptiness symbolized the presence of God more accurately than anything human hands could have shaped.

For Christians, God is present in Christ, and the history of Israel was a preparation for his coming. He is Emmanuel, God with us. He is God's "express image"[1] and we are to look at him to see what God is like. But the theme of absence recurs at, precisely, the crucial point. The moment at which we see most clearly the character of the God we worship is the moment of dereliction. When the Lord cried out, "My God, why hast thou forsaken me?", he bore, not unflinchingly but the more completely, the suffering of the world in which there often seems to be no sign of God. Without that absence we should not have the right to claim God's presence in the depth of affliction.

So in the Old Testament God's presence is symbolized by an emptiness. In the New Testament He is most profoundly present in human life when His absence is most felt, when the Son seems to be abandoned by the Father. So it is in keeping with this repeated theme of absence taken up into presence, that the Resurrection establishes the new availability of the Risen Christ when he is seen to have departed from mortal life.

So when the people we love or we ourselves depart, we can afford to let go. We do not have to mummify the body or hope against hope that the soul is immortal. Death is not to be by-passed but vanquished. It really is more than just falling asleep but is still in God's control.

Our tombs are all going to be empty eventually by the processes of nature. We need a miracle each. Christians believe that we have sufficient testimony that our God is able and willing to raise the dead. But we still need to ask, "With what body do they come? What can it mean to say that presence is renewed on the other side of real absence?"

We come back here to the place where the path forked,[2] back from the theologians to the philosophers. We may trust God to remake each of us, but what do we mean by this? Our reason for believing that God can raise the dead is that we believe He did. But if there is no separable soul to bridge the gap between this world and the next, nor any bodily continuity, what sense does resurrection make? What can this "remaking" be, on the other side of nothingness, in which we are to trust? Are the people in heaven going to be only copies, after all, of the people we know in this world? It is time to put the idea of a "pattern of lovability" to work, to show what it can do for us.

Copies of people?

The seed and plant analogy from St Paul and the Fourth Gospel[3] is, of course, only an analogy. It is an excellent corrective to really naïve ideas of resurrection. Christians have sometimes liked to picture the bodies of the righteous pushing their tombstones up and emerging as good as new. We need not be saddled with the idea that anything as naïve as that is what we are committed to as Christian believers. We do not have to think of those earliest fellow Christians who passed on the Gospel to us as simple people whose notions are embarrassing to our sophistication. The point of the seed and plant analogy is that the seed is transformed into the plant. One could not predict what would come up from looking at the seed. Our ideas of resurrection cannot possibly be adequate to the reality. "It does not yet appear what we shall be."[4] But we cannot push the analogy too far. Seeds growing into plants, or even grubs metamorphosed into butterflies, do not explain what our "metamorphosis" is to be when our bodies have entirely gone.

The difficulty that the idea of "patterns of lovability" hopes to meet has been called the "replica objection".[5] It is simply this, that once I have perished, body and soul, no remade copy of me will ever really be *me*. However convincing it looks, it will only be a replica of the real me, who will be dead. No continuity means no resurrection. The argument in the philosophical books and periodicals has gone on for a long time. In its most awkward form it points out that if it is copying we are talking about we are letting in again the notion of the multiple replication of a person. Why should there not be lots of copies of the one prototype? But the copies cannot all be me, especially when they have lived on for a bit and diverged from one another. But in that case not one of them is me. Any of them is as real, or as sham, as any other.

The appeal to the power of God is the answer, but we have to be careful not to cheat. If we just say something like, "As a matter of fact we are quite safe because God never would make more than one copy" we have not answered the logical difficulty that a copy is still only a copy. It helps, anyway, if we point out that the only reason we have for thinking that God will remake us at all is that He loves each individual one of us, and therefore any thought of lots of copies ought never to get started. But even a unique copy is not the original. More needs to be said about how the remade me really is me across the chasm of death.

The other half of the answer must be, "Well, why not?", but that is still more like assuming what is required to be proved. It is essential to be frank about the amount of weight which needs to be put upon the notion of "lovability" as the very nature of a person. The "same person" is not just any pattern which repeats the one that has gone, like a newly-knitted jumper. We are not talking about copies at all, but about what it means to be oneself. The heart of personal identity is mattering. Any discussion that leaves this out is "academic" in the negative sense, abstract and arid.

We are asking how I can hope to live again, on the assumption that I really do die, body and soul. We can ask it as a religious question about the grounds of our hope: "How can I get across this gap?" Or we can ask it as a philosophical question about personal identity:

"How can *I* get across this gap? Will it still be me?" The answer, both ways, has to do with my mattering. The religious answer is that I cannot, myself, get anywhere once I am dead. That is why talk of "immortal souls" is misleading. The only hope is for the person God loves to be renewed by God. The only continuity I have, or need, is God's continuing love for this "pattern of lovability". God's mercy can hold me in existence, not as just a dear memory, as the "process theologians" seem to say, but as something more like a blueprint ready to be rebuilt.[6]

We need the philosophical answer too because the notion of a mere replica is very persistent. Will it be me that reappears? But philosophy ought still to listen to common sense. Why after all must a resurrected person be "only a copy"? Suppose I *can* somehow (we have just said, by God's power) get across this gap, why should what appears on the other side *not* be I myself? Why must I produce a body or a ghostly soul as a passport, when the person who is me is not essentially either of these but a particular focus of minding and being minded about? If I come alive again after death, whatever hiatus there was will no longer signify. If it is me, I shall recognize myself with a particular kind of certainty which is not just intellectual: not "I think, therefore I am" but, as it were, "Here I am".

Some people may well say that what I mean by "pattern" is just what they mean by "soul". Some defenders of "souls" produce accounts very like this.[7] It becomes in a way a matter of terminology whether the concept of "patterns of lovability" is taken to be a denial or a defence of "souls". But there remains a significant difference of emphasis between the idea of an immortal spirit and the idea of a "mortal", entirely dependent upon a new embodiment which might be called miraculous.

If I believe that I really am mortal but that God can

raise me up, I can cope with the idea that in the meantime I may in fact be out of existence. It makes sense to think that I might look back upon death and understand that there was a time when I was nowhere, but that now I am myself again. And when there are other people who matter to me, I can recognize them after they have been nowhere, as easily as I can recognize them after they have been to Australia. If my friend has a twin I may have some difficulty. If the twins are playing tricks on me I may have a great deal of difficulty. But these are practical problems about identity. There is no worry about the theory. I know what recognizing the right twin means. I also know what it means to come to recognize someone who has changed "out of all recognition".

It would not be at all surprising if our resurrection bodies and behaviour needed drastic transformation. To recognize us in heaven may take much longer for the people we love than a walk to Emmaus. But what counts is that the characteristic pattern of the person, which is the way we are recognizable now through all our changes, should be able to come through. To identify the very same person is not to apply this or that test but to recognize the familiar pattern. People need tests only when they do not know each other very well.

Consecration

In using the idea of a "pattern" in this "value-laden" way[8] we have crashed the philosophers' fact/value barrier, not negligently, but in the hope of showing that it is both needless and hopeless to remove all that really matters from people and then expect them to survive. If personal identity can be entirely understood without bringing in the value of a person, it is no wonder that it seems too flimsy to last. But people are not interchangeable units coming off a factory line. Fact positively needs to be, as it were, thickened out with value. There is no need to look on people as "value-free". People as such call out some kind of response, positive or negative. I can be entirely neutral about a thing, but to be entirely neutral about a person, without interest or gratitude or animosity, just is to treat that person as a thing. We are so constituted that we do respond to other people. We hardly ever treat them merely as things, at least when we are aware of their immediate presence. To be jostled by a crowd is an entirely different experience from forcing one's way through undergrowth. When a human voice gives us a message we tend to say "thank you", even if it is really an answering machine.

The proper response to a person is indeed to give thanks, at many levels, from mild goodwill to devotion. At the best, we celebrate each other's existence. But now I may take one more rash step with my eyes open. Having tried to thicken out fact with value, let me try to thicken out both with theology. The Greek for "thanksgiving" is *eucharistia*. The combination of ideas, celebration, thanksgiving, presence, is itself for Christians a familiar pattern. We are used to giving thanks and finding presence, in a body which has been appointed. We believe we live in a world in which physical "elements" can be blessed into spiritual meaning. Can this give us a clue for understanding our own embodiment?

The point is that spirit needs body to be findable. Souls and bodies are not separable things mysteriously connected. Body is the way "soul" finds expression. People are embodied spirits. But when this emphasis on the body as our way of keeping in touch is combined with the idea that people are meeting points of fact and value, we have practically said that a person is a kind of sacrament, a place where spiritual reality is conveyed by physical reality. A sacrament is an "outward and visible sign of an inward and spiritual grace". So it is not a trick to say that we need bodies in order that we may indeed be "means of grace". If the world is charged with the grandeur of God, we can say that the human frame is charged with the grandeur of the lovable person.

Most human encounters may seem to fall a long way short of being "sacramental": but do they? When we begin to realize what is implicit in even the most casual dealings we have with one another we find ourselves on the edge of mystery. Generally we take the mystery for granted. We do not feel any particular awe at one another's presence, any more than people who do not happen to be convalescing from an illness are aware of feeling well. It takes a desert island to make Robinson Crusoe see a footprint as something marvellous. Ordinarily we overlook what a lot one is taking for granted in saying "Good morning" to the postman, let alone in opening the letters. Maybe a chipped flint in a museum will send us into a reverie about what it means to be human: but in fact almost every material object we can see, from fountain pen to window frame and the road visible through it, has been worked on by human hands. "There has been someone here" is, properly considered, astonishing, however it happens to be drawn to our attention. "There is someone here now" is the foundation of everything that gives life significance. The question about another life is how our presence is to be re-established.

Instead of saying that one day God will make a new copy of me, could we not say that He will consecrate a new body to be me? This is not a way of establishing resurrection to the satisfaction of sceptics: "Look, this is a sacramental universe, so that proves it." It is a way of finding words already familiar to us to explain what

110

resurrection could be. It is an attempt to show that in talking about resurrection bodies we need not be talking about mere replicas. The conviction this way of thinking tries to express is that any resurrection that makes sense is the special gift of God, controlled not only by logic but also by love, and in line with His revealed dealings with us. We may think of resurrection, then, as the fulfilment in which the pattern of each person shall again become presence, our own real presence of which we may each say (perhaps in surprised delight), "This is my body". So we may hope to be remade, and to find ourselves again as means of grace for one another.

FOR REFLECTION

S. T. Davis, "Is Personal Identity retained in the Resurrection?", *Modern Theology* 2:4 1986

You can't refute a theory merely by imagining possible worlds in which the theory would be exceedingly difficult to believe.

John Hick, *Death and Eternal Life*, Collins 1976, p. 285

Resurrected persons would be individually no more in doubt about their own identity than we are now, and would presumably be able to identify one another in the same kinds of ways and with a like degree of assurance as we do now.

John Austin Baker, *The Foolishness of God*, DLT 1970, p. 272

For where the human person has dissolved into nothingness only a new creation, in the strict sense of that word, can bring him back. And to create is something no one but God can do.

The First Epistle of John 3:2

Beloved, we are God's children now; it does not yet appear what we shall be, but we know that when He appears we shall be like Him, for we shall see Him as He is.

Presence Again

Julian of Norwich, *Showings*, Chapter 68

And these words: You will not be overcome, were said very insistently and strongly, for certainty and strength against every tribulation which may come. He did not say: You will not be troubled, you will not be belaboured, you will not be disquieted; but He said: You will not be overcome. God wants us to pay attention to these words, and always to be strong in faithful trust, in well-being and in woe, for He loves us and delights in us, and so He wishes us to love Him and delight in Him and trust greatly in Him, and all will be well.

And soon all was hidden, and I saw no more after this.

10

Purpose and Pointlessness

Doing and being

We project into heaven our best ideas about what
human beings are meant to be here on earth. So it is
high time to consider whether in all the argument
about "patterns of lovability" I have worked my way
into a dangerously one-sided emphasis. Have I
suggested an alarmingly activist and even arrogant
answer to the ancient question "What is man?"? A view
which loses sight of God's love for the unlovable cannot
be right for earth or heaven, and a liking for activity
which loses sight of quiet contemplation is at odds with
what some of the wisest human beings have taken to be
our true goal.

The argument so far has offered a decidedly
strenuous picture of human beings as God's creatures.
The idea of "soul-making" has been built upon the
concept that people do not start ready-made but are
shaped by living. They are active, practical strivers,
dynamic not static. It is the *living* God in whose image
they are made. This "activist" approach has been a
promising corrective to the theory of ghosts in
machines. It delivers us from out-of-touch "minds" with
unappreciated bodies. But deliverers turn into tyrants,
and correctives need counter-correctives. There is a
snobbishness of activity as much as a snobbishness of
intellect. Once we define people as essentially active
beings it is only a short step to judging people by the
success of their activities; and that is "justification by
works" in a particularly unmerciful form.

The idea of "soul-making" was supposed to deliver us from any notion that we are indestructible in our own right. We are mortal, body and soul, and need to be re-created by God's power, not our own. But the argument can be twisted round the other way. If souls are made by struggling actively towards maturity they seem to be in charge of their own salvation, whereas souls endowed with immortality by their Maker from the outset depend totally upon God. It may begin to look as if what is really valuable about us is an achievement rather than a gift. Does this matter? Gift or achievement, it is all by the grace of God; but as usual there is a question of emphasis.

The values of striving for achievement, earthly or heavenly, go along with an emphasis upon the glory of creation.[1] The values of receptiveness to the gifts of God go better with an insistence upon our absolute need for His mercy. Of course we require both. If we cannot quickly reconcile them at least neither ought to be silenced.

Achievement, like success, is an intoxicating notion, a mixture of excellence and danger. The danger is not that we are trying to steal God's glory. The more we appreciate the possible splendour of human creatures, the more we *ought* to be able to magnify God our Creator. But perhaps we shall never pause to do so. Then if heaven is one long pause we shall hardly find ourselves very well suited to it. It will be no wonder if some of the little ones whose achievement is modest or negligible find themselves more at home than the en-thusiastic activists who have forgotten how to notice anything but success, whether their own or other people's.

There are times when success is a kind of failure because it is too much shadowed by its cost. People screw themselves up to a high pitch of performance and lose sight of everything but the immediate struggle.

Then they need to be encouraged to relax and be less anxious, and to be reminded that it is not what they *do* but what they *are* that matters. In this frame of mind we set up Mary above Martha again, and quiet contemplation above stressful managing. It is all very well to be "dynamic", but if that shrinks to being merely busy we shall find ourselves idealizing busy bodies. It is all very well to give, but if we are all givers who are to be takers? What, after all, is activity for, in the end? Unless it comes to rest somewhere it is just self-perpetuating movement.

It is no wonder that at present the pendulum has a tendency to swing against the values of "activity". Conscious as we are of millions of people unemployed, we are more than usually ready to be told that life is not to be lived for the sake of achievement. "Who are you?" ought not to mean "What do you *do*?" in our eyes any more than in God's. Earthly economics seems to have put a question mark against our admiration for action and achievement, if it has conveyed a message of uselessness to so many people. Some Christians have readily recognized that the greatest problem is not how large numbers of people are to manage to live without paid work, but how they can value themselves when everyone has been accustomed to value people according to their jobs. So we have been trying to damp down our approval for paying one's way and playing one's part. The "Protestant work ethic" has come in for a good deal of blame for misleading us cruelly all these years. A different kind of Protestant emphasis seems more to the point: that there is no need to be justified by works and salvation is not to be earned.

The argument about activity can also be carried on in terms of "purpose". Like "activity", *purpose* is a word full of promise, both for morality and religion. Morally, if something is good one wants to know what it is good *for*. Religiously, the living God is the God with purposes. When He is "all in all" His purposes will all be fulfilled. But we cannot make "purpose" an end in itself, any more than we can make activity an end in itself. If we do, there comes a time when we have to say "And now what?"

John Stuart Mill in his autobiography tells the story of his strict upbringing according to the principles of his father, who was the first distinguished adherent of Bentham's utilitarianism. He grew up with a great sense of purpose, with "what might truly be called an object in life; to be a reformer of the world".[2] But he came to a crisis when suddenly he asked himself, "'Suppose that all your objects in life were realized; that all the changes in institutions and opinions which you are looking forward to, could be completely effected at this very instant: would this be a great joy and happiness to you?' And an irrepressible self-consciousness distinctly answered 'No!'."[3] He became profoundly depressed, and seemed to have nothing left to live for. Gradually but completely he recovered and learnt to feel enjoyment again. Most of all he was helped by the poetry of Wordsworth, who taught him that "there was real, permanent happiness in tranquil contemplation", and this without turning away from his fellow human beings.[4]

Thoughts like this may prepare the ground for a particular kind of emphasis on *pointlessness* which has been coming to the fore lately, not trivial pointlessness but a kind of high ethical pointlessness with an appeal both to religious and non-religious people. There is a reaction against the kind of utilitarianism that thinks it can always calculate benefits. We are being reminded from several directions that we ought not always to be asking "What is the use of it?" The fact that creation is not arranged for our convenience is being brought to our attention as exhilarating rather than regrettable.[5]

The Hope Of Heaven

Once upon a time Paley argued for the existence of God because the universe is so carefully constructed, like a well-made watch that could not have appeared without a maker. We have learnt so much since Darwin from scientists of all kinds about the working out of creation, that we can say, without having read Paley's book, that a rigidly purposive picture of God's ways will not do. The natural world is good for us to contemplate, not because it is all carefully contrived, still less because it is all laid on for our benefit, but just because of the splendour of its independence of our parochial human concerns. The distance of the galaxies, the millions of years before human life appeared, the depth of the oceans, the strangeness of the wilderness, are too great to be just a backcloth for our ups and downs. This has always been true, though now it has become obvious. Saint Augustine made the point: "It is the nature of things considered in itself, without regard for our convenience or inconvenience that gives glory to the Creator."[6] So activism is rebuked and contemplation comes into its own instead. We are invited to wonder, not at purpose but at pointlessness. An unselfish attention to what is entirely outside ourselves can be the beginning of worship, and could be a foretaste of heaven. If there is a message in nature it is not always "Keep struggling", but "Hush".

It is encouraging to be reminded that it is not only the great achievers who are made in God's image, and that to be capable of admiration and appreciation is a gift in its own right not a temptation to waste time. There is a tradition here. Whether we do or do not warm to the idea of "wise passiveness"[7], it is no new idea trotted out to comfort the unemployed. "Be still then and know that I am God"[8] is a much older corrective to strenuous fretfulness. Augustine, after all the arguments of *The City of God*, arrived at this point:

"We shall rest and we shall see; we shall see, and we shall love; we shall love, and we shall praise. Behold what shall be, in the end, and shall not end."[9]

Rest and work

There is a risk now of jumping to conclusions. How tempting to tell people who are unemployed that their condition is heavenly! How tempting to swing away from activity to *rest* as the key idea to unlock the problem of what a human being is for. Economics and theology suddenly seem to click together, and up comes the idea of *leisure* as a happy answer to our problems in this world and the next. But that is moving too fast.

Half-truths are more misleading than plain falsehoods. Contemplation really is nearly related to rest and leisure, and busy activity may obstruct it. But that does not mean that contemplation can easily solve the problems of enforced leisure, whether in this world for economic reasons or in our picture of the next world for pious reasons. It is cheating simply to identify "nothing to do" with leisure, and then identify leisure with contemplation.

Notoriously the Greek ideal of contemplation depended upon slaves. Even if the silicon chip can now be our slave, there is a big gap between millions of people without work and contemplation for all. Equally notoriously there are a great many people for whom compulsory leisure, as they experience it, means nothing like contemplation but at best bread and circuses. The idea of more free time may or may not be delightful, but it is not exactly the same thing as the meaning of life.

As long as leisure really means the absence of work, people who find themselves with a great deal of leisure will still think of themselves, triumphantly or despondently, as "not working". However energetically they occupy themselves, they do not have what their fellows call "a job". What they are as human beings, no longer related to what they do, remains related, even less happily, to what other people do and they do not.

It is all very well to say to a retired person, "Now you have time to pause and enjoy"; or to a workaholic, "You are missing the one thing needful". It is excellent to remember the dignity, even the Christ-likeness, of being a "patient".[10] It is worth defending people who dislike competitive rat-races. To all these we can truly say, "It is not what you *do* but what you are". But it is not so happy to say to redundant employees that their work is not wanted. To tell people that there is no need for them to do anything is apt to be as patronizing as it is untrue. To belittle achievement and excellence is, if not the sin against the Holy Spirit, at least a sin against the human spirit. It is all very well to understand that rest is not just idleness, only justified if it sets us up for more work. But it does not follow that rest is the "one thing needful" and work is only for the sake of winning through to rest.

Neither rest as an end in itself, nor work as an end in itself, seems to meet our needs as the real purpose of our existence. Can we tolerate as a happy state of affairs, or even approve as a thoroughly good state of affairs, the idea of a final achievement of purpose, of work done "for good and all"?[11] When activity stops, does inactivity take over for ever? The Sabbath follows six days of work but it also comes before six days of work. The Christian Sunday is the first day of the week, not the last. What has seemed good for us so far is a rhythm of work and rest.

We can look at John Stuart Mill's misery as pathological. But is this because we are always taking for granted that really there *is* still plenty to strive for? Could we bear the fulfilment of *all* our purposes? Browning's Childe Roland came to the Dark Tower feeling that he could not cope

"With that obstreperous joy success would bring"

and failure might be best. Goethe's Faust promised the devil that his soul should be forfeit the moment he felt totally satisfied. Both these answer to something in our experience. What we think of as an "end" has a way of turning out to be something we never reach, or worse, do not want when we have reached.

For some good people this whole argument may seem silly. We know what the "one thing needful" really is, far as we may be from reaching it. It is, of course, the Vision of God, which is utterly an end in itself. How could we imagine carrying on with any of our activities in God's presence? But to say that too quickly gives us the grown-up answer when we are, most of us, still babes. The idea of the Vision of God dazzles us and all we can discern is the notion that it will swallow us up in endless inactivity. Unless that negative picture is to prevail we must allow ourselves to go on asking the childish questions, knowing that they are childish. Will there be anything to do in heaven, or shall we just "wait around" dressed all in white, as we sing every year at Christmas time?

At least we can point out that we are already in God's presence and what we do may sometimes please Him. If we are destined to become entirely static, what has been the point of making us the dynamic creatures we are now? The Vision of God is meant to be for the children of God. If human creatures are being made for heaven, what does that tell us about heaven?

If the Vision of God is too dazzling for our eyes we may look about us in the hope that what we see will be illuminated by its light. What we want, in our naïvety, to know is whether our natural human wish to fill out our heavenly hopes with active as well as passive ideas is in order or not. We cannot hope to make progress towards an answer if we are in a muddle about what work and rest mean to us on earth. What is work? Is it a disagreeable necessity, God's punishment for sin? or is it the true fulfilment of a human being made in God's image? How fundamental is the idea of working for six days and resting on the seventh? Is heaven an endless Sabbath or an entering into divine activity? Is one's earthly work a sacred calling, however menial or tedious? There are many practical and theoretical attitudes we can take up, and the difficulty is to relate them to one another. On the front of Modena cathedral a Romanesque Adam and Eve apply themselves dolefully, and apparently half-heartedly, to tilling the ground. Less mythically, we learn that our earliest ancestors were hunter-gatherers and that this economy did not have to be an incessant search for food. They would have had more leisure than we have, leisure for hospitality and sociability. People who work in factories hate the machines that make them redundant, while people who work in kitchens are eager for the machines that give them free time. People with hobbies sometimes work harder than people with chores. Are we to say they are not "really working" because they are under no external compulsion? Is it work to read a novel one enjoys in order to review it? Is a business lunch work? How many hours' work a day does a housewife do? Can a clergyman say more truly than a layman that "to work is to pray"? It is not altogether a trivial matter if we find this kind of question muddling.

Suppose we accept that work at any rate is not an end in itself. Let us even define work as activity undertaken for a reason outside itself. It does not have to be an economic reason. Nor do we have to restrict work to what we do reluctantly. But if it is work it is done *for* something. Its central meaning is still the paid job one lives by, whether or not one enjoys or endures it, thinks it worthwhile or diminishing. Voluntary work done for an assortment of motives is work too. Housework is certainly work, again whether or not it is relished or hated. The drudgery necessary to artistic creation or scholarship are work, even if nobody is going to pay for the products. The slave whose master beat him was working, and so is the self-employed trader who drives himself. Children's homework is work. Learning a language is work. Digging in the garden is work, whether the gardener is a horticulturalist or a retired professional man.

So far, so good. It is at the next step that we have to avoid confusion. Work is taken on for all sorts of reasons, but we cannot say it is taken on for the sake of rest. We cannot make rest into the "end" for which work is the "means". It is clearer to say that rest makes sense only in relation to work. Rest is recuperation from work, and generally we rest in order to get ready for more work. We do not rest for the sake of rest, any more than we work for the sake of work. "Leisure" is more like an end in itself, but does not really stand up on its own. It is best characterized as the welcome or unwelcome lack of work. People with leisure are people who, at least for the present, have no work to do. Without work in the background leisure would lose most of its meaning. It cannot be the substance of heaven.

But then, if we are not mystics and find the idea of "contemplation" as our only end too static and too specialized, is there any way in which we can, not demote, but widen contemplation so as not to shrink our destiny to one way only of glorifying God? Of all the notions we have bandied about -- activity and passivity, work and rest, purpose and pointlessness -- the most seemingly unattractive, pointlessness, is after all best to put us on our way. It is surprisingly hard for us to grasp that not everything is for the sake of something else. To be able to tolerate what looks to us like pointlessness can be a way of seeing that the best answer to "What is the point of it?" may sometimes be, "It does not need a point outside itself: it is its own point". Here is a way into the tangle of ideas about "means" and "ends" which may presently help to put human striving in its proper place.

The idea we need as a contrast to work is not just something less strenuous. It certainly is not just something we do without wages. It is something we do for its own sake, which has all the point it needs within itself. If we have to have one word for this idea, the nearest is "play". Play is more positive than "leisure", less static than "rest". It is less lofty than "contemplation", perhaps not lofty enough to be the whole answer: but it can take us further than we may think. Playing can include working and resting, activity and appreciation, entertainment and invention; and above all it includes enjoyment.

Human beings, young and old, are playing animals. To play properly they have to lose some of their sophisticated self-consciousness. Christians have been told to become as little children, so they struggle to be innocent or to be obedient, taking these as the ideal qualities of childhood. But the most obvious characteristic of children is that they play, naturally and wholeheartedly, because that is what they enjoy doing. Children want to play instead of doing their homework, and to their parents and teachers homework is more important. Its point is obvious: it equips them for the future. The parents and teachers are right here and now, of course. If they let the children off the homework they are letting them down. But if they suppose that they are right eternally it is they, not the children, who have lost touch with real life. Playing is heavenly: it is the most telling image of heaven we have.

Play can be frivolous or even heartless, because we are not in heaven. We are among the troubles and sins of human life. What was wrong with Nero's fiddling was that Rome was burning. But playing rightly understood is a reminder of the glory of creation, "When the morning stars sang together and all the sons of God shouted for joy".[12] In the Jerusalem Bible the verse about Leviathan in Psalm 104 was translated: "Leviathan whom you made to amuse you."[13] To glorify God has a great deal to do with enjoying Him for ever,[14] and if we understand that this includes not taking our own selves too seriously, so much the better. We can hope to forget ourselves and take pleasure in the "pointless" existence of things that were not made for our convenience. The point, so to say, of pointlessness is not the vain uselessness of creation but its exuberant richness. Our delight in all this is not something we can earn, by harder and harder work or in any other way. Jürgen Moltmann described heaven as a round dance.[15] Surely becoming as little children can mean partly that we and our heavenly Father at last will play together for the sheer joy of it.

FOR REFLECTION

ed. Beach and Niebuhr, *Christian Ethics: Sources of the Living Tradition*, Ronald Press Co., New York 1955. Introduction to chapter on Puritan ethics

Every moment of time as lived under the shadow of eternity becomes "high" time, crucial time to be up doing the duties of one's job. "Be busy; the soul is at stake, so loiter not", writes Jeremy Taylor. One Puritan preacher forcefully phrases the matter: "They that will not sweat on earth will sweat in hell."

Anthony Bloom, *School for Prayer*, Libra 1970, p. 55

. . . One of the things which we must unlearn, is looking at the clock. If you are walking somewhere and are aware that you are late, you look at your watch. But you cannot walk as quickly while you look at your wrist as if you simply look straight ahead. And whether you are aware that it is seven minutes or five or three minutes, you are none the less late. So add a starting time and you will be there on time, or else if you are late, walk as fast and as briskly as you can. When you are at the door, have a look to see how contrite you must look when the door is opened! . . .

John Austin Baker, *The Foolishness of God*, DLT 1970, pp. 52–3

On what grounds do you call millions of light-years of inter-galactic space a "waste"? A waste of what? Of space? On this basis, in proportion, a hydrogen atom is a shocking example of waste, for that is mostly space – as are you and I for that matter.

Purpose and Pointlessness

Anyway, what is wrong with vastness? Is not a sense of splendour and excitement as sound a response to it as this time-and-motion tutting?

Iris Murdoch, *The Sovereignty of Good*, RKP 1970, p. 85
We take a self-forgetful pleasure in the sheer alien pointless independent existence of animals, birds, stones and trees.

It is important too that great art teaches us how real things can be looked at and loved without being seized and used, without being appropriated into the greedy organism of the self. This exercise of *detachment* is difficult and valuable whether the thing contemplated is a human being or the root of a tree or the vibration of a colour or a sound. Unsentimental contemplation of nature exhibits the same quality of detachment: selfish concerns vanish, nothing exists except the things which are seen. Beauty is that which attracts this particular sort of unselfish attention. It is obvious here what is the role, for the artist or spectator, of exactness and good vision: unsentimental, detached, unselfish, objective attention. It is also clear that in moral situations a similar exactness is called for.

W. Vanstone, *The Stature of Waiting*, DLT 1982, p. 114
God creates a world which includes among its infinite variety of wonders this culminating wonder – that there are points within it at which, in the consciousness of men, its wonders are received and recognized.

Thomas Traherne, *Centuries* No. 29
You never Enjoy the World aright, till the Sea it self floweth in your Veins, till you are Clothed with the Heavens, and Crowned with the Stars: and Perceiv your self to be the Sole Heir of the whole World: and more then so, becaus Men are in it who are evry one Sole Heirs, as well as you.

The Hope Of Heaven

St Augustine, *Confessions* XIII 37

In that eternal Sabbath you will rest in us, just as now you work in us. The rest that we shall enjoy will be yours, just as the work that we now do is your work done through us. But you, O Lord, are eternally at work and eternally at rest. It is not in time that you see or in time that you move or in time that you rest: yet you make what we see in time; you make time itself and the repose which comes when time ceases.

11

Fears and Hopes

Babes

Up to a point it is proper for Christians to be agnostic about heaven. To have anything of one's own to say about it suggests a dangerous brashness or even irreverence. What can we say, except that God will be all in all? If that sounds dreary, our total unworthiness for heaven is shatteringly exposed. The more we argue, the more we invalidate our own arguments.

And yet that is not all there is to be said, not as things are at present. If we were living in an "age of faith", then we should need to be ready to turn our backs upon our own vivid imaginings and attend to God Himself at the centre of everything: but our time is a time of doubt. Many people, many Christians even, are already so agnostic about God that they need more help. Our imaginations need feeding, not slimming.[1] To tell us that heaven is the vision of God and nothing but the vision of God is precisely like reminding children that grown-up people do not have teddy bears. Heaven seems to be the place where what we put our hearts into here will be taken away from us, and yet we are supposed to look forward to it. Indeed we are children at the moment: not like the child chosen out by the Lord to show who belongs in the kingdom,[2] but more like St Paul's "babes" who are used to milk and are being given platefuls of meat.[3] When a child says, "I don't want it" with a wrinkled up face, it is already too late to say, "Eat up your lovely dinner".

It need not be selfish or shallow to try to build up our

129

hopes, even with childish imaginings. "You will lapse into silence", said St Augustine, "if you lose your longing."[4] We shall do poorly if we outgrow the Psalms: "They shall be satisfied with the plenteousness of thy house: and thou shalt give them drink of thy pleasures, as out of the river."[5] We can hardly want to be so sophisticated as to outgrow the parables of the gospels with their recurrent theme of rewarding delight. Indifference is much worse than naïvety:

> Nothing offending he is all offence;
> Can stare at beauty's bosom coldly
> And at Christ's crucifixion boldly.[6]

We do not want to become people who do not care about anything, so we need to make sure that we are not squashing what we really care about in the name of piety. Our hopes and wants may be totally inadequate when they are brought out into the light of day, but they are sounder than an unreal official hope which is only covering up a deep-rooted fear.

The matter of boredom needs to be squarely faced. H.H. Price gently caricatured the notion that heaven is eternal hymn-singing. "No doubt the congregation would contain many very admirable persons, and it would be a pleasure, indeed an honour, to be singing in their company. But it did not seem to occur to religious teachers that a perpetual Sunday morning might become tedious after a while. One can have too much of a good thing."[7] The answer must be not to withdraw from the whole idea, but to vary the picture as the gospels do, putting in more not fewer images of what we find heavenly in human life.

There is no merit in being so negative about heaven as to lose touch with the idea that God means to delight us. On the contrary, we can take encouragement from those members of the Communion of Saints who have put their imaginations to work in the service of their fellow Christians. St Augustine, Julian of Norwich, Dante, Thomas Traherne, C.S. Lewis, Austin Farrer . . . these are some who have thought it right and fitting to hearten us with positive images of God's purposes. By filling in and enriching our hopes they are very far from turning us away from God.

But through the generations, alongside definite hopes, there have been equally definite appeals to fear. Taking God seriously must be partly a matter of giving thought to the idea of judgement; but it has to be admitted that human notions of divine judgement have often burgeoned uncontrollably. Human beings seem thoroughly to enjoy devising places of punishment and putting their enemies into them in God's name. Among the painters, only Fra Angelico seems to depict heaven more convincingly than hell. Nowadays we may worry that heaven would be tedious, but far more Christians down the years have worried that, far from boring us, God means to torture us. Let us say distinctly that both the tedium and the torments are human imaginations which come from mistaken ways of trying to exalt God. The doctrine of hell in some of its popular forms has been a real blot on the Christian faith.

No doubt divine judgement is under-emphasized today, in reaction against these perversions of it. It has become easy to assume, "Dieu me pardonnera: c'est son métier". But though God's wrath must be more, not less, awe-inspiring than we sometimes suppose, it cannot be sadistic if the Christian Gospel is to make any sense at all. Many Christians would gladly write off the whole idea of hell as an aberration, but are brought up short by the fact that there it is, very plainly, in the New Testament. A closer look gives some relief. The most alarming account of punishment, the rich man who ignored the poor man at his gate, is part of a parable.[8] It is serious but perhaps not literal, any more than "Abraham's bosom" has to be literal.

The vivid and recurrent images of fire and worms are primarily images of destruction. Gehenna is a rubbish heap not a prison. There are many such tips outside Mediterranean hill-towns to this day, where the rubbish is not preserved but consumed.

What we have to take seriously is the thought that we are capable of self-destruction. We might live in such a way that our "patterns of lovability" would eventually become too distorted, or too faint, to be able to persist. We have no guarantee of indestructibility. The rubbish heap might be the only place for us. Certainly we cannot be allowed to wreck heaven for other people. There are people who seem to spread hell around them, sometimes quite gently and even with charm but with horrible effect. In Marlowe's *Doctor Faustus* there is a compact statement of what it is to be diabolical. Faustus succeeds in summoning up the devil and enquires how it was that he could get out of hell: to which Mephistopheles replies, "Why, this is hell, nor am I out of it".[9] When one considers that kind of damnation one may well ask, "Lord, is it I?" But it is better to dwell upon the mercy of God and to hope, not sentimentally but reverently, that mercy will turn out to be the finally irresistible force against which nobody will be an immovable object.[10]

It is no wonder that purgatory has seemed a promising idea to human beings who hope for mercy but cannot believe that most of us are nearly ready for heaven. Here if anywhere agnosticism is in place. We dare not try to make plans for God, especially plans which turn legalistic as quickly as most notions of purgatory are apt to do. A safer speculation might be the idea that heaven need not be "all of a piece", that there might be development in blessedness and scope for more growing.

Surely there is no need to assume such a fixity in heaven that prayer for the dead is simply ruled out.

People naturally pray for their nearest and dearest, and if they find it still natural to go on praying for them when they have died, it is no less than cruel to require them to stop. Dead people are in God's hands as they were when they were alive. God will do His best for them, for ever. We cannot improve upon what God will do, but surely we may be allowed to try to associate ourselves with it? That is what it could mean to be human "means of grace". Perhaps we might even find that we had been allowed to give some kind of particular flavour of our own to the limitless blessing of God.[11] Prayer for the living is surely less puzzling seen in this way, and it seems quite promising to think like this of prayer for the dead too. At least we can get rid of any notion of buying or begging off their allotted penalties and negotiating them into heaven sooner. It does not seem too fanciful to imagine, less rigidly, that God might allow us to bless one another and even accept us partly for one another's sake. Praying for enemies has a place here; but more surprisingly, perhaps we could pray for saints as well as for sinners. Gratitude as well as forgiveness may be conveyed from one person to another. Of course this is not an idea to be snatched at glibly. If there remain a good many Christians whose ingrained Protestantism makes it seem more natural to remember the dead and give thanks for them, but not to try to make prayers on their behalf or belittle the gap death makes, such honest holding back can also be a worthy kind of Christian faith.

Maturing

We cannot imagine heaven: but it is defeatist to react so strongly against "other-worldliness" that heaven goes by default. We know that "eternal life" must be a quality of life now, rather than mere continuation in another world. To bring eternity into this life is much to be wished; and a warning against pseudo-scientific inquisitiveness could be salutary. We do need to be reminded that whatever eternal life is, it has something to do with a transformation which is supposed to start here, not with simply going on and on as we are after death. But as soon as the emphasis is fixed on this life only, so that the whole idea of another world is really belittled, then the Christian hope is put in mothballs.

What we need to keep it ready is not defensive and pedantic arguments which shrink our ideas, but live images, and especially images which make our inability to anticipate heaven into something positive. In relation to heaven we really are children, looking ahead to maturity but full of misconceptions about it. "When I am grown up I will eat as many sweets as I like and stay up past my bed-time." A grown-up life which perpetuated childish priorities would quickly pall.

In relation to the love of God we are even more like household dogs, lively members of the family but comprehending nothing like all that happens. A dog is thoroughly related to our world and even has a human vocabulary: dinner, walkies, down, on trust; but he cannot begin to describe our world in it, even when our proceedings concern him nearly. He sees the suitcases and knows something is going on, but has no idea what it means to pack for a journey, even if at journey's end he can chase a ball on a beach. His worship is partly cupboard-love, but surely transcends cupboard-love. He responds to happiness and sadness, he welcomes friends and tries to drive away enemies. He becomes almost human by human adoption and grace.

One more image relating this life to the next might be still more apt. An unborn foetus lives and moves and maybe has feelings. It has an ordeal ahead, by which it will enter an unimaginable world for which its present circumscribed existence is a preparation. Meantime it is nourished and grows, and arrangements of which it knows nothing are made to welcome its dramatic arrival. Surely we may take the teaching that we must be born again if we are to enter the kingdom of heaven to suggest some of these meanings of literal birth: struggle, newness, and joy.

If these images – the child, the dog, the foetus – help, it is because they are not attempts to say what heaven must be like, when really it is entirely unknown to us, but ways of saying something positive about the nature of our ignorance. The basis of our hope is that if we really are God's creatures, then heaven is what we are made for. If we can look at ourselves, who are not entirely unknown to us, as candidates for heaven, we can hope for a kind of sidelong. glimpse of what our destiny is meant to be.

What *are* these human creatures that God takes such pains to perfect? Here we have come back almost to where we began. The life of the world to come must arise out of what we, as God's creatures, are.[12] We are told we are made "in His image", and once upon a time that would have meant something simple enough: that we were shaped in His shape, maybe literally out of clay. Yet surely, at least as far back as we can trace our traditions, people have understood that there is poetry here. God is not shaped like a man: His image is not our physical shape but our rational and loving nature. That is what, we hope, is being perfected in us, with whatever expense of creative power and redemptive suffering.

FOR REFLECTION

John Burnaby, *The Belief of Christendom*, SPCK 1959, p. 194

This, we say, is what heaven would be for me; and when we hear of another man's dream of it, we say, If it is going to be like that, it is no place for me! – And so long as we are – no doubt unconsciously – prescribing to God the kind of heaven He must provide for us if we are to welcome the prospect of it, we are betraying our unfitness for the only possible heaven, which is a life of which God and not ourselves will be the centre.

The Venerable Bede (from his tomb in Durham Cathedral)

I implore you, good Jesus, that as in your mercy you have given me to drink in with delight the words of your knowledge, so of your loving kindness you will also grant me one day to come to you, the fountain of all wisdom, and to stand for ever before your face.

St Gregory of Nyssa, *The Life of Moses*, Classics of Western Spirituality, Paulist Press

. . . the continual development of life to what is better is the soul's way to perfection.

For the perfection of human nature consists perhaps in its very growth in goodness.

Austin Farrer, *Saving· Belief*, Hodder and Stoughton, 1964, p. 143

It is silly to say, "How marvellous to be in heaven! Our shirts will be whiter than the latest detergent can wash them, and we shall have no need to switch on the electric light." It is not silly to say, "Every now and then, perhaps, I manage to be at the disposal of God's will. How marvellous to be in heaven! I shall live in it all the time." Nor is it silly to say, "From time to time I think I catch a glimpse of what God is doing. How marvellous to be in heaven! I shall see His purposes in everything, as clearly as I read my friends' feelings on their faces." Nor is it silly to say, "Every now and then I see a bit of what God has put into the people round me. How marvellous to be in heaven! I shall see it all." Nor is it silly to say, "I acknowledge Christ by faith, and bless him in words for being very God and very man. How marvellous to be in heaven! I shall be familiar with the man in whom the Godhead is."

12

The Image of God

Paradise

In the Book of Genesis the statement that man and woman together are made in God's image is not part of the same story as the modelling of the first man out of clay.[1] There is not just one primitive legend but complex raw material here for Christian imaginations to work upon, or rather to play upon. If we take these ancient traditions not as fundamentalist history but as tantalizing inspiration there is plenty of nourishment to be sucked out of them. The "modelling" story reminds us of our twofold nature, physical and spiritual. The "image of God" idea is a foundation for our hopes that human nature has a divine value.

Christians who have been nurtured on the Scriptures are apt to be more fundamentalist than they realize. It is hard to give up the notion that whoever compiled the Book of Genesis must have meant something theologically important in every sentence. Would it be safer to give Adam and Eve a rest? It seems a pity to be so afraid of being childish that we pettishly refuse to find any inspiration at all. In an almost mischievous spirit, maybe we can preach a kind of sermon on an old-style text, quite seriously but not too solemnly. We can take the most naïve statement from these ancient stories and draw a certain combination of ideas out of it which may be a help in our would-be adult questionings.

Adam and Eve "heard the voice of the Lord God walking in the garden in the cool of the day".[2] We are surely safe from taking this primitive statement quite literally. We can use it as a kind of slogan to pick out three related ideas for the better understanding of our eternal hope, by way of a firmer grasp of what personality is, divine and human. There are certain things we can try to say both about God and about ourselves which can give us a glimpse of what we are made *for*.

First, there is the idea of God's voice. God has no vocal cords, whether or not the writer of this verse thought that He did. Surely the prophets who insisted "Thus saith the Lord" were not being so literal-minded. But they were vividly aware of a God who found ways of getting in touch with them.[3] The word of the Lord was a concept with a strong meaning. The God of our tradition is a God who communicates. To be made in His image is to be able to communicate with one another. Language has something to do with the essence of personality. It will surely continue to have something to do with the life of the Communion of Saints.

Secondly, there is the idea of the garden. God has no hands for digging in the earth, but the whole natural world takes its rise from Him. It is His nature to bring order out of chaos, and more than that, to bring to existence and cherish what was not there before, in intricate and wonderful detail. Gardens can be classical or romantic, formal or wild. There are nursery gardens and pleasure gardens; and there are gardens where the brambles take over. People have thought of the universe in all these ways. We may well say that the garden of which Adam is the gardener has not yet grown to its full stature, and that there is still a lot of work going on in it. St Paul expressed this by saying that "the whole creation has been groaning in travail together until now".[4] The point is that when we find people fulfilling their own natures by transforming bits of the creation, from homo habilis making tools nearly two million years ago, to Joseph the carpenter, or Michelangelo the genius, or our own do-it-yourself neighbours: then we are looking at small-scale models of God the Creator. Are we to say that creation, divine and human, is all over in heaven? The image of Paradise need not foreclose that question.

Thirdly, we must dare to say that God is capable of delight. In this too we may think of ourselves as like our Maker. Enjoying the cool of the evening is a more vivid picture than resting on the seventh day. In small Italian towns on summer evenings the whole population, especially parents and children, walk unconcernedly up and down the roads: a foretaste of heaven maybe, except for the traffic trying to nose its way through. The image of playing comes into its own here, not the only-too-serious hide-and-seek Adam and Eve begin to play among the trees, but the sort of cheerful holiday when people enjoy each other's company and laugh at the smallest joke.

Making

Most sermons preached about Adam and Eve have to be about sin. This one, more rashly, is about glory. Without forgetting human sinfulness, we may dare to take heed of the way that this ancient and primitive account from far back in our tradition allows us to hold certain ideas together, ideas we can take up as fundamental to what a person is: communication, creativity, enjoyment.

Is this whole picture altogether too "humanist"? "Communication" is all very well, but "creativity" and "enjoyment" both seem like rivals to Christian love. Creation seems to belong to God not to men, and enjoyment sounds individualistic and selfish. On the contrary: provided these ideas are kept together, they illuminate love and give it substance.

The Image Of God

All along we have been assuming that the creatures God makes and saves are worthwhile in His sight. This commits us to take creaturely glory seriously. If we do trace the image of God not only in loving but also in making we can make more sense of His purposes for us. Christian moralists are understandably wary when God's glory is allowed to include ours. We hardly dare think of human creatures as glorious. If they aspire to creativity, is that just a kind of pride or of self-indulgence? Is it safer to leave God to do all the making, and concern ourselves simply with loving? We are used to the idea of a great divide between the values of creation which we call "aesthetic" and the values of love which we call "moral". Must we accept that split, and make sure that we keep well on the moral side of it in creaturely obedience?

What God the Creator has made is a universe so immense that our minds cannot grasp it. We may well take it as an image of the glorious infinity of its Maker. But within that immensity we find ourselves, and we believe, not in stark arrogance, that finite as we are, we are the most authentic images of God. Austin Farrer said, "There is more theology to be dug out of a saint than out of a sandpit".[5] May the genius find a place alongside the saint? Whatever human beings may aspire to become, they are already makers. Their "mini-creativity" must be taken into account in consideration of what the "image of God" can mean.

Can "patterns of lovability" contain both artistry and unselfish love? This is no academic question but only too practical. Can the drive of a creative artist leave room for human kindness and affection? If that problem remains fundamentally intractable in this life, no wonder it makes havoc in our notions of a life to come.

We are not often going to meet the question in its so to say classic form: are we to rescue a drunken tramp or a picture by Raphael out of a burning building? But it

The Hope Of Heaven

is often an acute problem how far a talented person has the right, or even the duty, to neglect his or her family and ride roughshod over other people's feelings to pursue a clear vocation. Contemporaries may give one answer, posterity another. The outcome may seem to be a matter of "moral luck".[6] Is the work achieved important enough to justify the trail of misery it has left in its wake? Are creative people above morality? Or conversely, if love is everything, why worry about art? It sometimes seems impossible to believe that there is one right answer, even in God's sight.

The practical problems have to be wrestled with piecemeal, but something can be said to make them less absolutely intractable. If people are indeed made in the image of God who is both Creator and Saviour, then making and loving must be fully compatible. And after all, we can fit them together. The main point has to be that people are made for loving; but the story is not complete unless we give love a context; and that is where making comes into its own.

Suppose indeed that the point of a person is to love and to be loved, to mind and to matter; and at the best, to be happy and to give happiness. Then at once we have to add: one cannot just love or just mind, full stop. There has to be someone to love and something to mind about. Life needs raw material.

The world of things is the context in which all human loving is to be done, and we shape each other's worlds by what we do with things. Our Creator does not do all the making that is done for us. People make things for use; but also they make things for pleasure. They make tools and vessels, they make meals and clothes, they make houses and furniture, they make works of art "for art's sake". Sometimes all these activities are lucrative, often they are enjoyed. It is an essential fact about human making that from the earliest days the usefulness and the glory cannot be taken apart. Were the cave paintings sympathetic magic, part of the technique of hunting? Certainly the Solutrian laurel-leaf flints were more beautiful than they strictly needed to be.[7] We cannot date the origins of delight in workmanship. What we need to add is enjoyment of one another's artefacts, great and small, and we have made human creation as well as divine Creation the raw material of love.

Human creativity is not a lonely self-indulgence. There is no need to separate our making as something "vainglorious" from our loving as something "unselfish". "Art" and "morality" belong in the same world, not in two worlds whose values are characteristically at odds with one another. There are plenty of difficult clashes, just as there are among undoubtedly moral values like truth-telling and kindness. "May the artist neglect his wife?" is not a different sort of question from, "May the doctor deceive her patient for his own good?" Creativity is valuable, not in some separate sphere of "aesthetic" values, but in the same sort of way as generosity is valuable. These are not optional extras, sugar on the cake of moral duty. They are part of the stuff of a worthwhile life which love will impel us to try to bring into existence, not only for ourselves, but for one another. Enjoyment, including enjoyment of loveliness, has everything to do with morality in the end.

We can pick up again the notion of being allowed to be "means of grace" for one another. It is not too farfetched to think of the artist or the craftsman as a sort of priest, who takes some sort of physical "matter", which can seriously be called the elements of a sacrament, consecrates them and makes them available for communion.

"Communion" is a useful concept here because it does not fix any of us as active *or* passive. Making and contemplating are not two distinct roles, after all.

Appreciating is a positive activity, creative in its own way. Professor Gombrich has shown in fascinating detail what a lot of work is done by the beholder in realizing the meaning of a work of art. The most "realistic" painter is not making a straightforward copy of what he sees in a "take it or leave it" way. On the contrary, an enterprise is going on which makes demands on all concerned. We exercise our own imaginations and "share in the creative adventure of the artist".[8] Delight in creativity, even in somebody else's creativity, is not just fed to us as if we were battery hens.

We need not suppose that heaven is an enormous art class, whether for would-be professionals or for "Sunday painters", any more than it is an endless amateur choir. The point is that there are more ways than one in which the things we mind about on earth can be rehearsals for heaven, destined for fulfilment not for abandonment. It is still more to the point to say that the best rehearsal of all for heaven is to learn to delight each other. If we find that we continue to do this by making and showing one another things, that is just what we should expect if we believe we are made in the image of God the Creator.

We ought to stop thinking of love as unselfish but negative, and delight as positive but selfish. We can hold them together by firmly locating the "image of God" in our capacity to give each other delight. We can do this in many ways on earth, and surely more thoroughly in heaven.

Of course we dare not forget how defaced in earthly reality is the image we want to trace. Often we do not know how to delight each other, often we simply do not care, and sometimes we actually want to hurt each other. If there is a Creation, there certainly is some sort of Fall. There has to be re-creation in the sense of redemption before God's children can enjoy the recreation of the heavenly sabbath: before we can walk with Him in the garden in the cool of the day rather than hiding ourselves in shame at what we have been up to.

Both – and . . .

Heaven is play and maturity. It is body and spirit. It is love and fulfilment. We need not blur these contrasts, but hope to reconcile them.

For reconciling play and maturity, the image of rebirth helps. It suggests a kind of growing up into childhood, the innocence of a fresh start with the capability of a new stage. We have to be careful with the notion of innocence, as Christians have too often been thought to glorify immaturity and childishness. The innocence we need to fit us for eternal life is not naïvety but the innocence which makes a contrast with blasé cynicism.

What children are innocent of is looking at everything with an eye to something else, whether economic or social. They live in the present, spontaneously and wholeheartedly. They know that happiness is right; and the happiness of children is literally heavenly. Yet we are not to imagine that children are all alike. There is not one characteristic "childlikeness" to which we must all conform.

What we all have in common is that we cannot return to childhood by going backwards. To reach our new life we have to go on through death to rebirth. Death means letting go of everything, and for most of us that is a struggle. The best meaning of "dying daily" is not sternly mortifying ourselves but making a start on the necessary offering up of what we are now: getting ahead, as it were, with something which will have to be done thoroughly in the end.

If we are acquainted with any saints, we may feel

that they have begun their resurrection ahead of time, reconciling childhood and maturity. Their "unselfishness" is not lack of interest in little things but a kind of straightforward appreciation of essentials. They give us a kind of preview of what human life could be if it were restored to us set free of the ugly muddle grown-up people have normally accumulated.

A Christian heaven must also be able to reconcile body and spirit. The physical universe is surely not a dead end, but somehow or other will turn out to have been raw material for the ultimate purpose of God.[9] There are haunting suggestions in the Pauline epistles that nothing will be left out of the final reconciliation, since "all things hold together" in Christ who is "the firstborn of all creation" as well as "the firstborn from the dead".[10] The rebirth image is especially telling, for the picture of the whole creation "groaning in travail together until now" seems so true as to be hardly a metaphor. Is it only wishful thinking to hope that one day all nature will indeed be "set free from its bondage"?[11] These ideas have a robust tenacity which is not just starry-eyed. St Paul was no silly dreamer; and on the other hand there can be defeatist un-wishful thinking as obstinate as superstition.

Even physics takes its disciples well beyond sceptical common sense nowadays. If science is allowed to stretch our minds, theology is not to be ruled out just because it is wonderful. What we need for keeping our feet on the ground is a solid respect for real facts: our own embodiment, our dependence upon a physical context, the capacity of material things to serve as a vehicle for "spirit"; the insistent awareness of many down-to-earth people that earth is not everything; the tradition we have inherited of a God who makes and saves. The notion of an ultimately sacramental universe in which not bread and wine only but the whole physical world will be consecrated as an "outward and visible sign of an inward and spiritual grace" seems to give us a clue to reality rather than contradicting our experience.

The reconciliation of love and fulfilment is the most important because it is the reconciliation of each other. It ought to follow straight on from the unity of body and spirit. There would be no point in emphasizing our embodiment or the sacramental character of the material world in which we are placed unless we were placed in it together and were to find our fulfilment by "keeping in touch". Whatever heaven is, it surely is not the flight of the alone to the Alone, if this world is in any way a preparation for it. If a person is a "pattern of lovability", being a person has everything to do with relationships.

Heaven forbid that we should be carried away at this point by sentimentality. Realism tells us how far we are from heaven now. Fulfilment for ourselves and love of other people are still desperately at odds. Conflict, not Christian love, seems to be fundamental to our attempts to shape our lives. Human happiness is not just unequally spread but often positively based upon recalcitrant unfairness. We cannot pretend that people's interests are easily harmonized. Short cuts to heavenly peace are selfish or foolish or both.

What we have to encourage us cannot be short cuts, but foretastes. There are aspects of life as we know it that allow us to see that in principle fulfilment need not be "mine" to be snatched from you, and love need not be "yours" to be denied to me. Most of us can at least see what it is like to be truly pleased by someone else's pleasure or saddened by someone else's sadness. Human affections are not so corrupt that this equation has to be too difficult for them. Some people, lovers and parents for instance, can make a start with the sum already worked out for them.

An easy lesson in the heavenly mathematics is

giving a present to a friend. Giving and taking just do not have to be distinct and opposite. The happiness of a gift is not a happiness handed over from one person to another, less for him, more for her, but a reciprocal happiness growing out of the giving. Even when the gift is what we nowadays call a sacrifice, an offering that hurts, the happiness for both giver and recipient which will be harvested in the end will have something to do with reciprocal gladness and nothing to do with "quid pro quo". A real gift, small or large, is indeed a means of grace, and the grace flows both ways if it can.

The best images of heaven are images of hospitality. The idea of the heavenly banquet where God is our Host recurs throughout the New Testament and appeals to us at many levels: nourishment, pleasure, the exercise of skills, fun, formality, reward, welcome, reunion, celebration, offering and gratitude. This image of heaven as a feast is sacramental through and through. It is not at all a legalistic image, but nor is it undemanding. We may be "well-drest",[12] but we are not in uniform. Each of us is individually invited, and given the chance to enjoy each other's company. And we have to add: none of us has the right to walk in and demand service. The whole delight of the gathering is the limitless and marvellous generosity of the Host.

When we have encouraged ourselves with positive pictures to overcome our faint-heartedness it is time, not to dwell upon them but to put them carefully away in the back of our minds in case they should turn into idols. People who simply want to rebuild the agreeable life they know in heaven are, precisely, worldly. People who give themselves over to fantasies to compensate for the unhappy life they know are falsely "other-worldly". People who discount other people's earthly troubles and promise them heaven as a panacea or a placebo are putting themselves gravely under judgement. None of these are noticeably following the Lord who set his face to go to Jerusalem and found no short cut to by-pass the Cross. There is a great deal that we can rightly and hopefully tell ourselves and one another about resurrection; but always for Christians it must be triumph over death not escape from death.

FOR REFLECTION

St Paul, *Epistle to the Romans*, Chapter 6

Know ye not, that so many of us as were baptized into Jesus Christ were baptized into his death? Therefore we are buried with him by baptism into death; that like as Christ was raised up from the dead by the glory of the Father, even so we also should walk in newness of life. For if we have been planted together in the likeness of his death, we shall be also in the likeness of his resurrection.

The Shorter Catechism, Westminster Assembly

The end of man is to glorify God and enjoy Him for ever.

St Augustine, *Homilies upon 1 John* X:7

. . . The learning of charity, my brothers, its vigour, its flowers, its fruit, its beauty, its pleasantness, its sustenance, its drink, its food, its loving embraces – all these can never cloy. And if God grants us such delights upon our pilgrimage, what joys await us in our homeland!

Thomas Traherne, *Centuries* No. 42

But He Wanted Angels and Men, Images, Companions. And these He had from all Eternitie.

Barth and Brunner. V. Sproxton, Preface to Brunner, *Love and Marriage*

. . . even here there was a sharp distinction between Barth's and Brunner's tastes. Brunner was devoted to Bach. There was "nothing more heavenly beautiful than Bach's Double Violin Concerto". Barth's retort was that though the angels would probably have to play Bach on feast-days, when they were by themselves they would without doubt play Mozart.

Psalm 16

Thou shalt show me the path of life; in Thy presence is the fulness of joy: and at Thy right hand there is pleasure for evermore.

The Gospel According to St Mark, Chapter 10

With men it is impossible, but not with God: for with God all things are possible.

Notes

1. A Cluster of Questions

1. Psalm 104:24
2. Ibid. 31
3. Psalm 8:4–5
4. I have argued this at greater length in *The Hope of Happiness*

2. A Necessary End

1. *Julius Caesar*, Act II Scene 2
2. *Measure for Measure*, Act III Scene 1
3. Ecclesiastes 12:1
4. E.g. H.A. Williams, *True Resurrection*, Mitchell Beazley 1972
5. E.g. D.Z. Phillips, *Religion without Explanation*, Blackwell 1976
6. 1 Corinthians 15:19
7. Ibid. 15:35
8. I have argued this in an essay called "Mission, Morals and Folk Religion" in *Crossroads are for Meeting: Essays on the Mission and Common Life of the Church in a Global Society*, ed. Philip Turner and Frank Sugeno, SPCK/USA 1986

3. Doubleness

1. Matthew Arnold "Strew on her roses, roses"
2. Cf H.H. Price, Eddington Memorial Lecture 1953 "Some aspects of the conflict between science and religion", Cambridge University Press, pp. 53–4
3. Paul Badham, *Life after Death?* Forewords (Modern Churchmen's Union pamphlet No. 3) p. 12
4. Descartes, *Discourse on Method*. In *Body Mind and Death*, ed. Flew, p.129
5. Descartes, *Meditations VI*, ibid. p. 132
6. Descartes, *Meditations II*, ibid. pp. 130-1, 133
7. Hume, *A Treatise of Human Nature*, I:4:II
8. Cf A.G.N. Flew, "Selves" *Mind*, 1949, p. 355

4. Wholeness

1. Ryle, *The Concept of Mind*, p. 49
2. Ibid. p. 61
3. Ibid. p. 15

Notes

4. Strawson,
   *Individuals: an essay
   in descriptive
   metaphysics*,
   Methuen 1959, p. 104

5. Embodiment

1. *Hamlet* Act I Scene 2
2. "The Animals".
   *Collected Poems of
   Edwin Muir*, 1960,
   pp. 207–8, quoted by
   kind permission of
   Faber and Faber.
3. *Tractatus Logico-
   Philosophicus* 5.6
4. In this paragraph I
   am paraphrasing
   what I argued in
   *Incarnation and
   Immanence*, Hodder
   and Stoughton 1973,
   pp. 26–8
5. 1 Corinthians 15:35
6. Strawson, *Individuals*,
   pp. 115–16
7. 2 Corinthians 5:2–3
8. Psalm 115:17
9. *The Odyssey* Book XI,
   tr. Rieu, Penguin, p.
   177

6. Presence

1. I have discussed this
   problem in
   *Incarnation and
   Immanence*
2. See J.A.T. Robinson,
   Exploration into God,
   SCM 1967
3. Matthew 10:29
4. Oxyrhynchus papyri
5. Deuteronomy 30:14
6. Acts 17:27–8
7. Hebrews 1:1–2
8. Exodus 3:1–6
9. Isaiah 6:1–8

10. *School for Prayer*,
    DLT 1970, p. 1
11. The catechism, *Book
    of Common Prayer*
12. Mark 14:22 and 1
    Corinthians 11:24.
    See Mark 6:41; Luke
    24:30; John 21:13
13. Quoted in Rupp, *The
    Righteousness of God*,
    Hodder and
    Stoughton 1953, p.
    314
14. George Herbert "The
    Elixir"
15. Shakespeare Sonnet
    LXV
16. See Austin Farrer,
    Saving Belief, Hodder
    and Stoughton 1964,
    pp. 144–5
17. Described in W.
    MacDougall,
    *Abnormal
    Psychology*, and
    discussed in C.D.
    Broad, *The Mind and
    its Place in Nature*,
    Kegan Paul 1925. A
    similar case was
    described in *The
    Three Faces of Eve*,
    Thigpen and
    Cleckley, Secker and
    Warburg 1957

7. Patterns of Lovability

1. E.g. John Hick, *Death
   and Eternal Life*,
   Chapter 15
2. John 20:15–16
3. *Confessions* XIII:9
4. See David Jenkins,
   The Glory of Man,
   e.g. pp. 2–3, 96, 99
5. April 1819. Letter
   123. (p. 336 in O.U.P.

edition ed. M.B.
Forman 1935). See
John Hick, *Evil and
the God of Love*,
Macmillan 1966, p.
295; and on Irenaeus
6. See entry in *New
Dictionary of
Christian Theology*,
SCM 1983
7. Cf Helen
Oppenheimer, *The
Hope of Happiness*,
pp. 93–4
8. See an interesting
article called
"Augusta Ada and
the Religious
Education Problem"
by William Gosling,
in the St George's
House (Windsor)
Annual Review 1982
9. I return to this in
Chapter 9 (Presence
Again)
10. p. 104 below

8. The Resurrection

1. Mark 12:26–27
2. E.g. G.W.H. Lampe
in Lampe and
Mackinnon, *The
Resurrection*
3. 1 Corinthians 15:3–8
4. See above, p. 89
5. Acts 2:27; 13:35
6. 1 Corinthians 15:20
7. Luke 7:11–17; John
11:38–44; 2 Kings 4
8. E.g. Luke 24:39
9. John 20:15
10. Luke 24:16
11. 1 Corinthians 15:50
12. Ibid. 15:36. John
12:24
13. Mark 16:6; Matthew

28:6; Luke 24:3, 5;
John 20:2, 13
14. E.g. Barnabas
Lindars, "Jesus
Risen: Bodily
Resurrection but no
Empty Tomb"
Theology, March
1986 (and letters in
July)
15. John 20:17
16. Luke 24:31
17. Luke 24:51; Acts 1:9
18. 1 Corinthians 15:37
19. Ibid. 15:44

9. Presence Again

1. Hebrews 1:3
(Authorized Version)
2. Above, p. 86
3. Above, pp. 97 and 101
4. 1 John 3:2
5. Above, p. 85
6. Or again, like
software: see above,,
p. 85 and note 8 there
7. E.g. Paul Badham in
*Christian Beliefs
about Life after
Death*, pp. 93–4
8. See above, pp. 15 and
77

10. Purpose and Pointlessness

1. See above, p. 17
2. J.S. Mill,
Autobiography, 1873,
O.U.P. (World's
Classics) p. 112
3. Ibid. p. 113
4. Ibid, p. 126
5. See Iris Murdoch,
*The Sovereignty of
Good*, RKP 1970, e.g.
pp. 65–6, and the
famous passage about
the kestrel, pp. 84–5

Notes

6. *City of God* XII 4 (p. 476 in Pelican translation)
7. Wordsworth "Expostulation and reply"
8. Psalm 46:10
9. *City of God* XXII 30
10. W.H. Vanstone, *The Stature of Waiting*, DLT 1982
11. Cf Jürgen Moltmann, *Theology and Joy*, SCM 1973, p. 55
12. Job 38:7
13. Changed now in the New Jerusalem Bible (1985) to "whom you made to sport with"
14. The Shorter Catechism of the Westminster Assembly
15. *Theology and Joy*, p. 55

11. Fears and Hopes

1. I have said more on these lines in Chapter 19 of *The Hope of Happiness*
2. Matthew 18:1–6
3. 1 Corinthians 3:1–2
4. *On the Psalms.* Discourse on Psalm 37 (Our 38:9)
5. Psalm 36:8
6. "Indifference" Edwin Muir, *Collected Poems*, p. 50, quoted by kind permission of Faber and Faber
7. *Essays in the Philosophy of Religion*, OUP 1972, p. 84
8. Luke 16:19–31
9. Act I Scene 3
10. This is movingly argued by J.A.T. Robinson in *In the End, God*
11. I suggested this in an article in *Theology* on "Petitionary Prayer", February 1970, p. 64
12. See above, p. 27

12. The Image of God

1. Genesis 1:27 and 2:7
2. Ibid. 3:8 (Authorized Version)
3. See above, pp. 54–5
4. Romans 8:22
5. *A Science of God?*, Bles 1966, p. 17
6. Bernard Williams, *Moral Luck: Philosophical Papers 1973–80*, Cambridge University Press 1981
7. N.K. Sanders, *The Pelican History of Prehistoric Art*, Platel 1968
8. *Art and Illusion*, Phaidon 1960, p.278
9. Cf C.F.D. Moule, Ethel M. Wood Lecture 1964 "Man and Nature in the New Testament", Athlone Press
10. Colossians 1:15–20
11. Romans 8:18–24
12. George Herbert "Prayer is the Church's banquet"

155

Some Further Books

St Augustine, *Confessions*
Paul Badham, *Christian Beliefs about Life after Death*,
  Macmillan 1976
Paul and Linda Badham, *Immortality or Extinction?*
  Macmillan 1982
John Austin Baker, *The Foolishness of God*, DLT 1970
Bishops of the Church of England, *The Nature of
  Christian Belief* (pamphlet) Church House
  Publishing 1986
O. Cullmann, *Immortality of the Soul or Resurrection of
  the Dead?* Epworth 1958
Dante, *Paradiso*
C.H. Dodd "The Communion of Saints" and "Eternal
  Life" in *New Testament Studies*, Manchester Univer-
  sity Press 1953
James D.G. Dunn, *The Evidence for Jesus*, SCM 1985
Austin Farrer e.g. "Into the Hands" in *A Celebration of
  Faith*, Hodder and Stoughton 1970
ed. Flew, *Body Mind and Death* (selected readings),
  Macmillan 1964. (Especially Descartes, Locke,
  Butler, Hume)
John Hick, *Death and Eternal Life*, Collins 1976
Edgar N. Jackson, *The Many Faces of Grief*, SCM 1972
David Jenkins, *The Glory of Man* (Bampton Lectures),
  SCM 1967
  What is Man? SCM 1970
Johanson and Edey, *Lucy: The Beginnings of
  Humankind*, Granada 1981
Julian of Norwich, *Showings*
G.W.H. Lampe and D.M. MacKinnon, *The Resurrec-
  tion: a dialogue arising from broadcasts*, Mowbray 1966

Some Further Books

C.S. Lewis e.g., *The Great Divorce*, Bles 1945
   "The Weight of Glory" printed in
   They asked for a Paper, Bles 1962
John McManners, *Death and the Enlightenment*, OUP
   1985
Mary Midgley, *Beast and Man: the roots of human
   nature*, Harvester 1979
Jürgen Moltmann, *Theology and Joy*, SCM 1971
Helen Oppenheimer, *The Hope of Happiness: a sketch
   for a Christian humanism* SCM 1983
ed. D.J. Enright, *The Oxford Book of Death*, OUP 1983
Terence Penelhum, *Survival and Disembodied Ex-
   istence*, RKP 1970
Gilbert Ryle, *The Concept of Mind*, Hutchinson 1949
Cicely Saunders, Dorothy H. Summers and Neville
   Teller, *Hospice: the living idea*, Arnold 1981
Thomas Traherne, *Centuries*
W. H. Vanstone, *Love's Endeavour, Love's Expense*,
   DLT 1977
   The Stature of Waiting, DLT 1982

Index

Index

Index